The Collector's Guide to the Minerals of New York State

Dr. Steven C. Chamberlain
and Dr. George W. Robinson

Schiffer Publishing Ltd

4880 Lower Valley Road • Atglen, PA 19310

Cover Photo: Millerite. Sterling Mine, Antwerp, Jefferson Co. 4 cm. Smithsonian Institution (NMNH). CC

Other Schiffer Books on Related Subjects:
Collector's Guide to the Feldspar Group. Robert J. Lauf. ISBN: 978-0-7643-4329-2. $19.99
Collector's Guide to Fluorite. Arvid Eric Pasto. ISBN: 978-0-7643-3193-0. $19.99
Collector's Guide to Silicate Crystal Structures. Robert J. Lauf. ISBN: 978-0-7643-3579-2. $19.99
Collector's Guide to the Axinite Group. Robert J. Lauf. ISBN: 978-0-7643-3216-6. $19.99

Copyright © 2013 by Dr. Steven C. Chamberlain and Dr. George W. Robinson

Library of Congress Control Number: 2013931113

Designed by Mark David Bowyer
Type set in Snell Bd BT / Aldine 721 BT

ISBN: 978-0-7643-4334-6
Printed in China

Schiffer Books are available at special discounts for bulk purchases for sales promotions or premiums. Special editions, including personalized covers, corporate imprints, and excerpts can be created in large quantities for special needs. For more information contact the publisher.

Published by Schiffer Publishing, Ltd.
4880 Lower Valley Road
Atglen, PA 19310
Phone: (610) 593-1777; Fax: (610) 593-2002
E-mail: Info@schifferbooks.com

For the largest selection of fine reference books on this and related subjects, please visit our website at
www.schifferbooks.com.
You may also write for a free catalog.

This book may be purchased from the publisher.
Please try your bookstore first.

We are always looking for people to write books on new and related subjects. If you have an idea for a book, please contact us at
proposals@schifferbooks.com

In Europe, Schiffer books are distributed by
Bushwood Books
6 Marksbury Ave.
Kew Gardens
Surrey TW9 4JF England
Phone: 44 (0) 20 8392 8585; Fax: 44 (0) 20 8392 9876
E-mail: info@bushwoodbooks.co.uk
Website: www.bushwoodbooks.co.uk

Contents

Foreword from the Series Editor 4
Acknowledgments 5

Chapter 1: Introduction, Collectors, Geology,
and Types of Mineral Occurrences 6

Chapter 2: Occurrences in Sedimentary Rocks 15
    Herkimer Diamond Localities 15
    Minerals of the Lockport Dolostones 23
    Chittenango Falls Celestine Occurrence 29
    Alden Pyritized Fossil Locality 32
    Ilion Travertine Locality 33

Chapter 3: Occurrences in Crystalline Rocks 36
    Tilly Foster Iron Mine 36
    Amity-Edenville Area, Orange County 40
    Natural Bridge Titanite Occurrence 44
    Rose Road Wollastonite Occurrence near Pitcairn 46
    Bush Farm Brown Tourmaline Locality 50
    West Pierrepont Tremolite Occurrence 52
    De Kalb Gem Diopside Locality 56
    Russell Danburite Occurrence 58
    Pierrepont Black Tourmaline Occurrence 61
    Overlook Quarry 68
    Bedford Pegmatites 70
    Greenfield Chrysoberyl Locality 72

Chapter 4: Occurrences in Fractures 74
    Rossie Lead Mines 74
    Muscalonge Lake and Macomb Fluorite Occurrences 78
    Yellow Lake Road Cut 80
    Sterling Iron Mine 82
    Chub Lake Hematite Prospect 86
    Zinc Mines of the Balmat-Edwards Mining District 89
    Ellenville Mine 94

Foreword from the Series Editor

This Schiffer Earth Science Monograph presents the mineralogy of New York State, an area that is rich in history, geological variety, and "classic" occurrences. Mining is an important industry in New York, with economic deposits of talc, iron, zinc, limestone and dolomite, garnet, and wollastonite to name a few. The graphite deposit at Ticonderoga is memorialized on the pencils we all used as school children.

Mineral collectors worldwide are familiar with chondrodite from the Tilly Foster mine, and with the superb doubly-terminated quartz crystals known as Herkimer Diamonds. Scientists have described twelve new mineral species from localities in New York, from warwickite in 1838 to fluoro-potassichastingsite in 2005.

The authors are eminently qualified to introduce collectors to this fascinating subject. Dr. Chamberlain has been publishing research in mineralogy for thirty-five years. He is a specialist in New York minerals and serves as the volunteer coordinator of the Center for Mineralogy at the New York State Museum. Dr. Robinson has been a leading mineralogy curator for thirty years, first at the Canadian Museum of Nature and now at the A. E. Seaman Museum at Michigan Tech. A native New Yorker, he has specialized in its minerals.

—Robert J. Lauf

Acknowledgments

Producing this book has been a labor of love based on many decades of collecting, studying, and writing about the minerals of New York State. We are grateful to the many fellow collectors, mineral dealers, and research colleagues who, over many years, have helped us increase our understanding of New York minerals and localities.

We specifically want to acknowledge special assistance from our external Schiffer editor, Dr. Robert Lauf, and our internal Schiffer editor, Jeff Snyder. Michael Hawkins, the Collections Manager at the New York State Museum, never tired of answering our questions about the New York State Collection. We are indebted to the many mineral photographers, specifically listed below, for providing us with their images and giving us permission to use them in this book. We also acknowledge the many field collectors who found and preserved the specimens featured herein.

We thank Dr. Marian Lupulescu, Curator of Geology at the New York State Museum, for sharing his unpublished detailed analyses of tourmalines from New York State and providing the appropriate names under the new nomenclature guidelines. We also thank Marian for reading the final draft of the text for factual accuracy. His numerous suggestions and corrections improved the quality of the final version. We thank Dr. David Bailey of Hamilton College for his ongoing assistance with our mineral identification efforts. Dr. Helen Chamberlain did our final editing and proofreading before this book was submitted to the publisher, and we sincerely thank her.

Finally, we are particularly grateful to our wives, Helen Chamberlain and Susan Robinson, for their encouragement for us to undertake this project and their unflagging support until it was completed.

Photo Credits: CC–Chip Clark; ER–Eric Rutnik; GBG–George & Barbara Gearhardt; GWR–George W. Robinson; JAS–Jeffrey A. Scovil; JS–Jack Sheckerman; MH–Michael Hawkins; ML–Marian Lupulescu; MW–Michael Walter; RB–Ron Barber; SCC–Steven C. Chamberlain; and SN–Stephen Nightingale. Note that all sizes are maximum dimensions.

Collectors: The following is a partial list of the people who collected the specimens illustrated in this book: Schuyler Alverson, George Ashby, Charles Bowman, Chuck Bowman, David Bowman, Larry Bowman, Donald Carlin, Jr., Perry Caswell, Steven C. Chamberlain, William S. Condon, Tom Dillon, William P. Dossert, Adam Geer, Bill & Viki Hladysz, Terry Holmes, Nancy Koskie, Adrian LaBuz, John Leonard, Ivan McIntosh, Dave Millis, David Nace, Chester D. Nims, Vernon Phillips, George W. Robinson, Kenneth Rowe, Vern Sawyer, David Seaman, Ronald Waddell, Scott Wallace, Jay Walter, and Michael Walter.

Chapter 1
Introduction, Collectors, Geology, and Types of Mineral Occurrences

This book is an overview of the minerals found in New York State that are of interest to collectors. The rocks of New York are richly mineralized, and our presentation will necessarily be synoptic rather than comprehensive. While the state lacks any single locality that has produced hundreds of species, many of which are new to science, such as the quarries at Mont Saint-Hilaire, Québec, Canada, or the zinc mines at Franklin, New Jersey, there are, nonetheless, twelve mineral species that were first discovered and described from New York, starting with warwickite in 1838 and continuing into the present with the most recent being fluoro-potassichastingsite described in 2005. These species for which New York is the "type locality" are shown in the accompanying table.

Minerals First Described from New York State (Type Localities)			
Mineral	**Date**	**Locality**	**County**
Warwickite	1838	Warwick	Orange County
Edenite	1839	Edenville	Orange County
Clintonite	1843	Amity	Orange County
Manasseite†	1941	Amity	Orange County
Geerite	1980	Town of De Kalb	St. Lawrence County
Donpeacorite	1984	ZCA #4 Mine, Balmat	St. Lawrence County
Turneaurite†	1985	ZCA #4 Mine, Balmat	St. Lawrence County
Brewsterite-Ba†	1997	Valentine Property, Harrisville	Lewis County
Fluoropargasite	2003	Edenville	Orange County
Parvo-mangano-edenite	2004	Arnold Pit, Fowler	St. Lawrence County
Parvo-mangano-tremolite	2004	Arnold Pit, Fowler	St. Lawrence County
Fluoro-potassichastingsite	2005	Greenwood Mine	Orange County

†Indicates co-type locality

In 1969, the legislature designated garnet as the official New York State Gemstone. Untold tons of this mineral, much of it quite gemmy, have been mined in the vicinity of Gore Mountain in Warren County for use in abrasives for many years. The state also has produced significant quantities of iron, zinc, limestone, dolomite, rock salt, talc, and wollastonite.

At present, the legislature is in the process of designating the Herkimer diamond variety of quartz as the official New York State mineral. This is particularly appropriate since it is widely known, and there is a vast supply of the material, with many collecting sites open to the public. It is also probably the earliest mineral from the state that was appreciated for the beauty of its crystals, since the Mohawk Indians were collecting and using them for exchange long before the arrival of European settlers.

A number of significant works on New York minerals have been previously published. In Dr. Samuel Robinson's 1825 listing of mineral localities in the United States and Canada, New York occurrences already merited 45 pages. Dr. Lewis Caleb Beck's *Mineralogy of New-York* was the first state-wide mineralogy when it was published in 1842 and was detailed and comprehensive. Dr. Herbert P. Whitlock published a geographically arranged list of New York mineral localities in 1903, and in 1978, David Jensen published an extensive state mineralogy arranged alphabetically by mineral species. The present authors published listings of the gemstone and mineral specimen localities in the first New York State issue of *Rocks & Minerals* in 2007.

In this book, we present localities selected to illustrate the diverse and rich tapestry of New York minerals. Both historic, classic localities and modern localities are included. Moreover, we have grouped them not geographically, but by geological mode of occurrence. For each locality we discuss its significance, location and history, geology and origin, most important minerals, similar occurrences, and provide a list of cited references. Please note, that although we provide the precise GPS coordinates for every locality we discuss, this is not a field guide, but rather a guide for mineral specimen appreciation.

Fig. 1. Garnet is the New York State Gemstone. This 9 mm faceted stone was cut from gem rough collected at Gore Mountain in Warren Co. New York State Museum. SCC

Fig. 2. The Herkimer diamond variety of quartz may soon become the New York State Mineral. This 3 cm crystal with black anthraxolite inclusions was collected near Middleville, Herkimer Co. Jay Walter collection. MW

Collector History

Dr. Oren Root, a professor of mathematics, mineralogy, and geology at Hamilton College, assembled the earliest comprehensive collection of high-quality minerals from New York State. His collection was given to Hamilton College and is now on long-term loan to the New York State Museum. Chester D. Nims was an early mineral dealer specializing in the minerals of northern New York. Many specimens he collected and sold entered Root's and other nineteenth century collections. Dr. Albert H. Chester was on the faculty of Hamilton College after Oren Root. He was both a mineral collector and dealer. His collection of very high quality specimens, including many from northern New York, was given to Rutgers University. Dr. Silas R. Horton assembled an important collection of the minerals of Orange County that included specimens from the earlier regional collections of his father, William Horton; J. P. Young; and Dr. James Heron. His collection was subsequently dispersed. James G. Manchester assembled a fine collection rich in minerals from New York City and gave it to the public library of Fall River, Massachusetts. Recently, the Manchester collection was dispersed by the mineral dealer, Lawrence H. Conklin. Dr. Charles Upham Shepard assembled large collections of minerals, including many from New York. His first collection was purchased by Amherst College, but was destroyed by a fire in 1880. His subsequent collection was divided between Amherst College and the Smithsonian Institution.

In the twentieth century, the number of mineral collectors specializing in New York State grew. Elmer B. Rowley assembled an important collection rich in both display specimens and specimens of scientific interest. His collection is now in the New York State Museum. The late John N. Trainer's extensive collection of minerals from the Tilly Foster Iron Mine is also now in the New York State Museum. Ronald E. Januzzi also is an avid student of the same locality and built an extensive collection of Tilly Foster specimens. David E. Jensen's collection was a fine general collection with some very nice New York State specimens. His collection is largely at the Buffalo Museum of Science. William S. Condon assembled a collection, mostly of minerals from northern New York, now at the New York State Museum. The Ronald Waddell collection, at the New York State Museum, also has many important specimens from New York. Charles L. Bowman was one of the most active and expert field collectors in northern New York during the twentieth century, and like C. D. Nims, many specimens he collected entered contemporary collections.

Present-day collectors of New York State minerals include Schuyler Alverson, the authors, Stephen Nightingale, and Michael Walter, although there are many more. The best specimens from the Alverson and Chamberlain collections are in the New York State Museum, and those from the Robinson collection are in the Canadian Museum of Nature. Stephen Nightingale is assembling a collection especially rich in historic specimens from New York. Michael Walter is an active field collector and dealer. His own collection contains many fine-quality, self-collected specimens, but many more fine specimens he has collected have entered the collections of others.

Fig. 3. Dr. Oren Root, shown here in a portrait from the Hamilton College Archives, assembled one of the earliest and best collections of New York State minerals.

Geology

Any detailed discussion of the geology of New York State is well beyond the coverage of this book; instead, we will only summarize aspects of the geology essential to an understanding of the rock environments in which mineral specimens of interest to collectors occur. Several more detailed presentations of the geology are given in the references.

As the simplified map shows, New York State has two major kinds of rocks exposed at the surface—sedimentary rocks and crystalline rocks. Long Island is not shown because it is largely made up of unconsolidated glacial sediments with only a few small rock exposures on the surface.

Western and Central New York are covered at the surface by a coherent series of sedimentary rocks—sandstone, conglomerate, shale, siltstone, limestone, dolostone—that are youngest at the Pennsylvania border

and become progressively older toward the north. Sedimentary rocks also occur along the St. Lawrence River. All these rocks formed between 520 and 360 million years ago and include representatives in the Cambrian, Ordovician, Silurian, and Devonian Periods. Unlike the folded Appalachian Mountains to the south, the sedimentary layers in New York are largely flat-lying, but dip slightly to the south. Virtually all of the surface topography has resulted from glaciation and erosion rather than from tectonic events.

Northern and Eastern New York, the Adirondacks, and the Hudson Highlands have much older crystalline rocks exposed at the surface. These formed 1300 to 1000 million years ago and consist of various metamorphic and igneous rocks. Because of their great age, more weathering-resistant minerals, and complex history, the surface topography in these areas is much more rugged with higher relief.

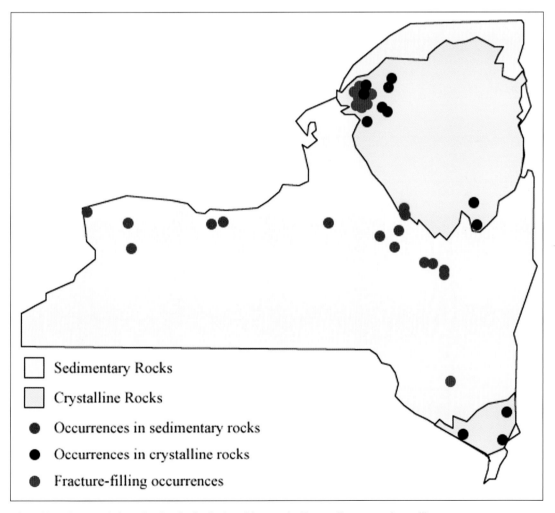

Sedimentary Rocks

Crystalline Rocks

● Occurrences in sedimentary rocks

● Occurrences in crystalline rocks

● Fracture-filling occurrences

Fig. 4. Map of New York State showing the distribution of the most significant sedimentary and crystalline surface rocks as well as the locations of the three types of mineral occurrences featured in this book.

Types of Mineral Occurrences

The organization of mineral occurrences that follows is based on their geological origins. At least in New York State, this provides some constraints on what sort of mineral species one might expect to find and emphasizes similarities among occurrences of similar type. Our classification includes three types of occurrences: those bedded in sedimentary rocks, those in crystalline rocks, and hydrothermal fracture-fillings. Some occurrences may have mineralization that actually fits into two different categories. In those cases, we have restricted our discussion to whichever category hosts those minerals of greatest interest to collectors.

Occurrences bedded in sedimentary rocks

Some minerals form in sedimentary rocks as the sediments themselves are being transformed into rocks (diagenesis). Other minerals form in empty spaces called solution cavities or vugs. These cavities, which are created after the sedimentary rock has formed, are often restricted to particular layers. Because conditions of sedimentation and subsequent diagenesis are often similar over relatively wide areas, many of the occurrences in this category represent geographical clusters of closely related occurrences in the same sedimentary rocks.

Fig. 5. *A strata-bound occurrence in sedimentary rocks. Exposures of many layers of flat-lying sedimentary rock at the Chittenango Falls celestine locality. Celestine occurs in solution cavities found in particular layers of this rock. SCC*

Fig. 7. *This 8 cm cluster of parallel calcite crystals formed in a solution cavity confined to a specific layer of dolostone exposed by quarrying near Norfolk in St. Lawrence Co. Steven C. Chamberlain collection. SCC*

Fig. 6. *An 11.9 cm cluster of pyrite crystals from a road cut on Interstate 81 south of Syracuse in Onondaga County. Here, pyrite crystals form flattened arrays parallel to the layers of limestone in which they occur. Steven C. Chamberlain collection. MW*

Occurrences in crystalline rocks

Crystallized minerals that occur frozen in metamorphic and igneous rocks are a very diverse group. Which minerals form depends critically on the conditions present, such as temperature and pressure, the chemical elements available locally, the presence of fluids, and time. Since most crystalline rocks in New York State are approximately one billion years old, successive stages of regional metamorphism, tectonic activity, and igneous intrusions have produced some very interesting possibilities for mineral collectors. Most such

occurrences are usually fairly limited in geographical extent, frequently measured in tens of meters or less, largely because the raw materials from which the minerals formed were equally limited in extent. Some metasedimentary rocks, however, like the talc-tremolite schists in St. Lawrence County or the marbles in Orange County may contain similar metamorphic minerals over wider areas because of their sedimentary origins and exposure to similar conditions of temperature and pressure during regional metamorphism.

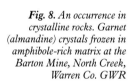
Fig. 8. An occurrence in crystalline rocks. Garnet (almandine) crystals frozen in amphibole-rich matrix at the Barton Mine, North Creek, Warren Co. GWR

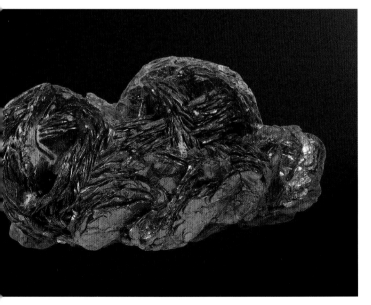

Fig. 9. This 8 cm specimen of graphite crystals was collected from crystalline rocks at Leib's Moonstone Mine near Bloomingdale in Essex Co. It is one of the finest specimens of crystallized graphite known. New York State Museum. SCC & ML

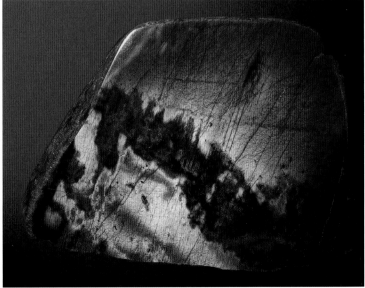

Fig. 10. A 9.5 cm polished specimen of labradorite collected from crystalline rocks (anorthosite) near Panther Pond near Harrietstown in Franklin Co. This variety of plagioclase feldspar makes an attractive gemstone when it shows a prominent play of colors. New York State Museum. SCC

Fig. 11. This 11.7 cm pargasite specimen was collected from crystalline rocks (marble/calc-silicate contact) on the O'Brien Farm in St. Lawrence Co. Steven C. Chamberlain collection. MW

Occurrences in fractures

Fractures in rocks result from the stress of tectonic activity. Faults are a common result. Weaker and more brittle rocks break more easily than those that are more ductile, and the fractures or faults produced may show similar orientations and patterns over many miles, reflecting regional stresses. What, if any, minerals form in spaces opened by fractures in rocks depends on the availability of mineralizing solutions. Sometimes these solutions invade a region producing a series of related fracture-filling mineralization with similar age and mineral composition, for example the Rossie-type lead veins in St. Lawrence County and adjacent Ontario. In other cases, the mineralizing solutions are very local, producing spatially restricted occurrences. Like mineralization in cavities in sedimentary rocks, mineralization of open fractures often produces crystallized minerals of outstanding clarity and perfection.

The following three chapters discuss mineral localities representing each of these three categories of occurrence. The selected localities all have produced excellent mineral specimens, but the representation is by no means exhaustive. The locations of the featured localities are shown on the map (Fig. 4), differentiated by mode of occurrence.

Fig. 12. This 5.5 cm fluor-dravite specimen was collected from crystalline rocks (granitic rock) exposed in a road cut on Cream of the Valley Road near Gouverneur in St. Lawrence Co. This is one of the best examples of this newly named tourmaline species yet found anywhere. Steven C. Chamberlain collection. SCC

Fig. 13. An occurrence in fractures: this is the entrance to an adit that followed a fracture-filling quartz vein at the Ellenville Mine in Ulster Co. GWR

Fig. 15. *This 1017 carat faceted calcite was cut from a flawless calcite crystal found as a fracture filling in marble in the Zinc Corporation of America #3 Mine near Balmat in St. Lawrence Co. A. E. Seaman Mineral Museum. GWR*

Fig. 14. *The stone chimney at the old workings on the Victoria Vein near Rossie in St. Lawrence Co. A number of parallel mineralized fractures were mined for lead in the early and middle nineteenth century. GWR*

Fig. 16. *This specimen of twinned calcite is 7.5 cm. It was collected from a mineralized fracture found in marble exposed in a quarry in Jefferson Co. west of Natural Bridge. Canadian Museum of Nature. GWR*

References

BAILEY, D. G. (2007) Geology of New York, the Empire State. *Rocks & Minerals* 82:464-471.

BECK, L. C. (1842) *Mineralogy of New-York.* W. and A. White and J. Visscher, Albany. 356p.

CANFIELD, F. A. (1923) *The Final Disposition of Some American Collections of Minerals.* Privately published, Dover. 20p.

CHAMBERLAIN, S. C., BAILEY, D. G., ROBINSON, G. W., and WALTER, M. (2008) Three historic New York mineral collectors: Oren Root (1803-1885), Elmer B. Rowley (1909-1992), David E. Jensen, (1909-1983). *Rocks & Minerals* 83:220-223.

CHAMBERLAIN, S. C., LUPULESCU, M. and ROWE, R. (2008) Discovery of fluorine-dominant dravite near Gouverneur, St. Lawrence County, New York. *Rocks & Minerals* 83:320-326.

JENSEN, D. E. (1978) *Minerals of New York State.* Ward Press, Rochester. 220p.

ROBINSON, G. W. and CHAMBERLAIN, S. C. (2007) The gems of New York State. *Rocks & Minerals* 82:458-463.

ROBINSON, G. W. and CHAMBERLAIN, S. C. (2007) Gazetteer of major New York State mineral localities. *Rocks & Minerals* 82:472-483.

ROBINSON, S. (1825) *A Catalogue of American Minerals, with their Localities.* Cummings, Hilliard, & Co., Boston. 316p.

WHITLOCK, H. P. (1903) New York mineral localities. *New York State Museum Bulletin 70.* 108p.

Chapter 2
Occurrences in Sedimentary Rocks

This chapter presents detailed accounts of five occurrences hosted in sedimentary rocks. The first three are examples of mineralization of stratabound solution cavities (i.e. the cavities are confined to particular layers): Herkimer diamond localities, minerals of the Lockport Dolostones, and the Chittenango Falls celestine occurrence. The fourth occurrence, the Alden pyritized fossil locality, is one where the mineralization took place during burial and diagenesis, while the final occurrence represents ongoing mineralization in a sequence of shales—the Ilion travertine locality.

Herkimer Diamond Localities

Significance

The transparent flawless crystals of quartz commonly known as Herkimer diamonds are one of the most sought after minerals from New York State (NYS) and almost certainly the best known. The Herkimer diamond is on track to become the NYS mineral through legislative action in the near future. The quality of the crystals, their abundance, and the large number of collecting localities open to the public make these quartz crystals of interest to beginning and advanced collectors alike.

Fig. 17. *Quartz. Herkimer Diamond Mines Resort, Middleville, Herkimer Co. 5 cm. Canadian Museum of Nature. JAS*

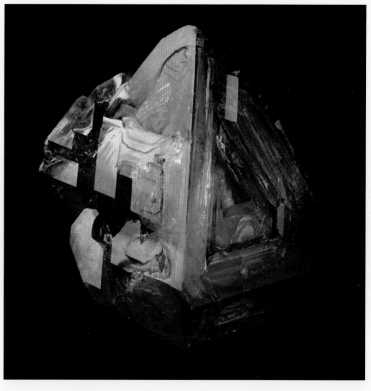

Fig. 18. *Quartz. Middleville, Herkimer Co. 9 cm. New York State Museum. ER*

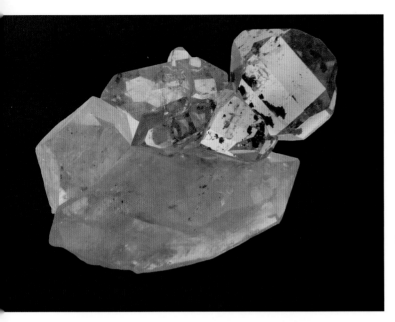

Fig. 19. Quartz. Herkimer Diamond Mines Resort, Middleville, Herkimer Co. 9.5 cm. Steven C. Chamberlain collection. SCC

Fig. 21. Quartz. Ace of Diamonds, Middleville, Herkimer Co. 11.5 cm. Steven C. Chamberlain collection. SCC

Fig. 20. Quartz. Ace of Diamonds, Middleville, Herkimer Co. 11.5 cm. Steven C. Chamberlain collection. SCC

Fig. 22. Quartz, calcite. Middleville Quarry, Herkimer Co. 2.9 cm. Bill & Viki Hladysz collection. MW

Fig. 23. Sceptered quartz crystal with calcite. Treasure Mountain, Little Falls, Herkimer Co. 9.5 cm. Michael Walter collection. MW

Fig. 24. Pale smoky quartz crystal with inclusions of anthraxolite. Treasure Mountain, Little Falls, Herkimer Co. 3.2 cm. Steven C. Chamberlain collection. SCC

Fig. 25. Black-stemmed, sceptered quartz crystals. Treasure Mountain, Little Falls, Herkimer Co. 10.3 cm. Uli Bauman collection. JAS

Fig. 26. Sceptered quartz crystals. Treasure Mountain, Herkimer Co. 9 cm. Steven C. Chamberlain collection. MW

Fig. 27. Black-stemmed, sceptered quartz crystals. Treasure Mountain, Herkimer Co. 7 cm. Steven C. Chamberlain collection. SCC

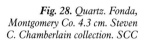

Fig. 28. Quartz. Fonda, Montgomery Co. 4.3 cm. Steven C. Chamberlain collection. SCC

Location and History

Multiple layers in the Cambrian-aged Little Falls Dolostone and the Galway Formation are mineralized with transparent quartz crystals. While anywhere either of these formations outcrops in the Mohawk Valley in Herkimer, Fulton, and Montgomery Counties may be considered a potential collecting site, eight localities have produced the majority of the specimens.

Herkimer Diamond Mines Resort (43°07'49"N, 74°58'32"W) is a fee locality open to the public west of NYS Rt. 28, south of Middleville in Herkimer County, NY. This was formerly known as Schrader's, Van Atty's, and the Herkimer Diamond Development Corporation.

Ace of Diamonds (43°07'56"N, 74°58'27"W) is another fee locality open to the public located immediately adjacent to the Herkimer Diamond Mines Resort property and was formerly known as the Petrie, or Tabor farm.

Middleville Quarry (43°09'14"N, 74°58'42"W) is a large, intermittently-worked quarry east of NYS Rt. 28, north of Middleville in Herkimer County, NY.

Treasure Mountain (43°02'09"N, 74°50'50"W) was a fee locality open to the public on Fall Hill overlooking the Mohawk River and the city of Little Falls in Herkimer County, NY. It is now closed. This was formerly known as the Parmon and Pederson farms.

St. Johnsville Quarry (42°59'58"N, 74°41'25"W) is an operating quarry north of US Rt. 5, west of St. Johnsville in Montgomery County, NY. Collecting may be permitted during occasional open houses. It has been variously known as the Talarico quarry, Eastern Rock Products quarry, Benchmark quarry, and Hanson quarry.

Diamond Acres (42°57'46"N, 74°28'13"W) is a fee locality open to the public along Stone Arabia Road, west of Fonda in Montgomery County, NY. This was formerly known as the Hastings farm.

Hickory Hill (42°56'33"N, 74°28'13"W) is a fee locality open to the public on several weekends each year along Hickory Hill Road, west of Fonda in Montgomery County, NY. This was formerly known as the Barker farm.

Crystal Grove (43°03'05"N, 74°38'02"W) is a fee locality open to the public east of County Rt. 114, west of Lasselsville, Fulton County, NY.

Herkimer diamonds were collected by Native Americans, especially the Mohawks, long before the arrival of Europeans. As Dean Snow points out about the Mohawks:

> They were known to themselves and to the other Iroquois nations as the Kanyenkehaka, the people of Kanyenke (also spelled Ganienkeh). This has usually been translated "Place of the Flint," but the flint (or more properly chert) sources in Mohawk country were not particularly sought after. More important were the clear quartz crystals now called Herkimer diamonds, which could be quarried in a few local mines and abound on Mohawk village sites. These were highly valued by Iroquois and other nations. Kanyenke was more likely "Place of the Crystals." Crystals were symbolically important as amulets of success, health, and long life, artifacts more likely to inspire a name than a second-rate chert. The Mohawks were the main suppliers of quartz crystals up to 1614. After that they became primary middlemen for the Dutch glass beads that replaced them. (Snow 1996, 43)

Lewis Caleb Beck described the occurrences in some detail in 1842:

> HERKIMER COUNTY. Uncommonly beautiful specimens of rock crystal, perfectly transparent, have been found in various parts of this county, especially at Middleville, Fairfield, Little-Falls, Salisbury and Newport. They are found sometimes in cavities in the calciferous sandstone; and at others, they lie loosely in the sand, probably produced by the disintegration of the rock. Mr. Vanuxem has remarked, that there is probably no locality in the world which produces more perfect or more beautiful quartz crystals than Middleville; and with an equal refractive power, they would rival the diamond. They are found of various sizes, and variously grouped. Perfect crystals have seldom been found here of more than two or three inches in length, while those of three quarters of an inch to an inch are also very abundant. They frequently contain specks and small masses of a black substance, which is believed to be anthracite … It is proper to state, that the occurrence of quartz crystals in such abundance in this county was first made known to the public by Prof. J. Hadley, of the Geneva Medical College. (Beck 1842, 261-262)

Because the quartz crystals are so abundant in the mineralized layers, each time large-scale excavations encountered these layers, articles appeared in the popular press. In the 1820s, when the Erie Canal was excavated through Little Falls, many Herkimer diamonds (then referred to as Little Falls diamonds) were encountered. In the 1880s as the railroad was built north to Middleville, the blasting of cuts between the road and West Canada Creek near the present fee collecting localities produced showers of perfect quartz crystals that were widely reported in the newspapers. Herkimer diamonds were sold for many years as souvenirs on the passenger trains of the New York Central Railroad.

Today, collecting Herkimer diamonds at the various fee localities is a notable part of the tourist industry in the Mohawk Valley. The Internet abounds with information and photographs of Herkimer diamonds, including whole websites dedicated to these exceptional quartz crystals.

Geology and Origin

Herkimer diamonds occur in vugs in both the Cambrian Little Falls Dolostone and the Galway (Theresa) Formation. At sites where many feet of rock are exposed, such as Fall Hill south of Little Falls or the Middleville and St. Johnsville quarries, it is clear that not all layers are equally mineralized and, while multiple distinct layers of mineralization exist, they are often separated by significant thicknesses of barren dolostone.

Some vugs are small, barely large enough to contain one or two quartz crystals. Others, such as those encountered in the St. Johnsville quarry, are several meters across. At the localities just south of Middleville, one layer contains dome-shaped pockets representing fossil algal stromatolites that usually contain many crystals and crystal groups. In all cases, the pockets include varying amounts of the carbonaceous mineraloid, "anthraxolite," which is also frequently present as inclusions in the quartz crystals. Similar mineralization is also present in certain dolostone units of the Beekmantown Group in St. Lawrence County.

Theories about how these quartz crystals formed abound: for example, that they formed from westward-moving solutions driven by the Taconic orogeny to the east. A recent theory that accounts for many observations, both in the field and of individual crystals, is based on the recent finding that certain organic acids can hold silica in solution, even under surface conditions. It is likely that the original carbonate sediments, which would eventually become dolostone, contained large amounts of both silica sand and organic matter that was subject to breakdown by bacteria, releasing organic acids capable of dissolving and holding silica in solution. Increasing temperatures caused by progressive burial under younger sediments resulted in gradual thermal splitting of the organic molecules holding the silica in solution. The slow crystallization from a subsaturated solution produced quartz crystals of exceptional clarity and perfection and also trapped fluid inclusions whose characteristics are consistent with the proposed mode of formation. Maximum temperatures were achieved during the Carboniferous period, which is probably when most of the quartz crystals were formed. Subsequent erosion of the overlying sedimentary rocks exposed the crystal-bearing layers at the surface.

Minerals

Herkimer diamond quartz crystals typically occur with dolomite, calcite, pyrite, marcasite, and goethite. However, except for the Middleville and St. Johnsville quarries, accessory minerals at the other localities are typically of poor quality and will not be described in detail here. The Middleville quarry has produced attractive amber calcite crystals and fine gray, white, and pink dolomite specimens. The St. Johnsville quarry has produced large quantities of very fine yellow and amber calcite crystals of complex habit with phantoms, associated with dolomite and rods and sheets of iron sulfides, now altered to goethite.

The various habits of quartz crystals found at Herkimer diamond localities are described below. Because of the enormous number of specimens that have been produced from these localities, generalizations about what occurs where always have exceptions.

Quartz, SiO_2, occurs as transparent, colorless to gray, milky, or pale brown to almost black crystals. Some of the more important habits are described below.

Single crystals are often colorless and flawless with minor or no attachments and few inclusions if they are less than 2 cm. More rarely, such crystals to 4 cm or slightly larger are found. Such single crystals can be found at all of the localities listed above, but are most common at the Herkimer Diamond Mines Resort and Ace of Diamonds, south of Middleville, and Diamond Acres, west of Fonda.

Isolated groups of transparent colorless crystals often are found in pieces and must be reassembled. Such unattached crystal clusters may contain from two or three to several dozen individual crystals and range in size to 30 cm or more. Such clusters appear to be most common at Herkimer Diamond Mines Resort, Ace of Diamonds, and Diamond Acres.

Matrix specimens of transparent colorless crystals occur in two types: as one or more flawless crystals trapped in a vug, the entirety of which is usually extracted as a specimen without freeing the crystals; or as flawless quartz crystals firmly attached to a matrix of darker-colored drusy quartz, which tend to be more abundant at Crystal Grove, Diamond Acres, and occasionally Herkimer Diamond Mines Resort.

Large crystals occur at all the localities, but are particularly common at Diamond Acres, Ace of Diamonds, and Herkimer Diamond Mines Resort. Large crystals to 20 cm or more are typically heavily fractured and appear gray or white rather than colorless. Crystals weighing over 9 kg have been reported.

Fig. 29. Quartz. Fonda, Montgomery Co. 17 cm. Steven C. Chamberlain collection. SCC

Fig. 30. Black-stemmed, sceptered quartz. St. Johnsville Quarry, St. Johnsville, Montgomery Co. 4 cm. Bill & Viki Hladysz collection. SCC

Skeletal crystals are often large (to 10 cm), and light or dark smoky brown. The skeletal faces are almost always the triangular rhombohedral faces rather than the prism faces. Most skeletal crystals formed attached to matrix, although many become detached by the time they are collected. Ace of Diamonds and Herkimer Diamond Mines Resort are noted for producing smoky skeletal crystals. The St. Johnsville quarry produces many gray skeletal crystals.

Black-stemmed scepters are the least common and, therefore, among the most desired habit of Herkimer diamond. A black prismatic stem is topped by a colorless, larger, crystal at the tip. Only two localities have produced significant numbers of these scepters: Treasure Mountain and the St. Johnsville quarry. Sometimes these occur in clusters of several attached scepters and as matrix specimens with calcite and dolomite.

Similar Occurrences

Nedrow thrust fault (42°57'28"N, 76°08'11"W); Warthone quarry near Perryville (43°01'07"N, 75°48'31"W); Jamesville witherite locality (42°59'11"N, 76°02'30"W); Barrett quarry near Norfolk (44°46'52"N, 74°59'29"W); Diamond Island in Lake George (44°46'52"N, 74°59'29"W); cement mines in the Rondout formation near Rosendale (41°50'33"N, 74°05'50"W).

References

BENNETT, P. C. (1991) Quartz dissolution in organic-rich aqueous systems. *Geochimica et Cosmochimica Acta* 55:1781-1797.

BENNETT, P. and SIEGEL, D. I. (1987) Increased solubility of quartz in water due to complexing by organic compounds. *Nature* 326:684-686.

BOROFSKY, R. L., WHITMORE, R., and CHAMBERLAIN, S. C. (2000) Scepter Quartz Crystals from the Treasure Mountain Diamond Mine near Little Falls, Herkimer County, New York. *Rocks & Minerals* 75:231-23.

CHAMBERLAIN, S. C. (1988) On the origin of "Herkimer diamonds." *Rocks & Minerals* 63:454.

CHAMBERLAIN, S. C., and HLADYSZ, W. J. (1997) Black-stemmed 'Herkimer Diamond' scepters from Fall Hill, Little Falls, Herkimer County, New York. *Rocks & Minerals* 72:121.

DOSSERT, W. P., and CHAMBERLAIN, S. C. (1991) "Herkimer diamond-like" quartz mineralization and calcite twins in the Marcellus shale near Syracuse, Onondaga County, New York. *Rocks & Minerals* 66:41-42.

FAST, J. B. (2008) A 2007 collecting venture in Herkimer County, New York: Thirty-eight quartz pockets. *Rocks & Minerals* 83:196-200.

HADLEY, J. (1832) *New-York Medical and Physical Journal.* p 132.

HLADYSZ, W. J., HLADYSZ, V. J., and CHAMBERLAIN, S. C. (1997) Black-stemmed 'Herkimer Diamond' scepters from the Eastern Rock Products Quarry, St. Johnsville, Montgomery County, New York. *Rocks & Minerals* 72:125.

JONES, B. (1976) Herkimer diamonds. *Rock & Gem* 6:20-26, 76-77.

JONES, B. (2009) Crystals so gemmy they're called "diamonds." *Rock & Gem* 39:12-16.

KAPELEWSKI, J. A. (2009) Tales from decades of Herkimer diamond digging. *Rock & Gem* 39:22-25.

LA BUZ, A. L. (1969) The "Herkimer diamond" grounds. *Rocks & Minerals* 44:243-250.

MITCHELL, J. R. (1982) Field trip: Herkimer diamonds—Six locations where you can dig New York's quartz "diamonds." *Rock & Gem* 12:62-67.

SNOW, D. (1996) *The Iroquois.* John Wiley & Sons, New York. 271p.

TUTTLE, D. L. (1973) Inclusions in "Herkimer Diamonds," Herkimer County, New York quartz crystals. *Lapidary Journal* 27:966-976.

ULRICH, W. (1989) The Quartz Crystals of Herkimer County and its Environs. *Rocks & Minerals* 64:108-122.

VANDERBILT, H. L. (1985) Herkimer diamonds. *Lapidary Journal* 39:45-47.

WALKER, D. and WALKER, C. (1990) Herkimer "diamonds." *Lapidary Journal* 44:71-72.

WALTER, M. (2004) Diamond Acres: Hunting New York's spectacular Herkimer diamonds. *Rock & Gem* 34:64-66, 68-69.

WALTER, M. (2007) *Field Collecting Minerals in the Empire State.* Privately published. 212p.

Minerals of the Lockport Dolostones

Significance

Well crystallized minerals in cavities in Lockport Dolostone provide elegant mineral specimens from sites all long its extent from Niagara Falls eastward to Clinton, NY. Although most of the species provide fine specimens, crystals of fluorite and sphalerite in various colors are generally the most sought after by collectors.

Location and History

The various members of the middle-Silurian Lockport Group have a total thickness of about 200 feet at Niagara Falls and become progressively thinner toward the east until they vanish east of Clinton in Oneida County, NY. Everywhere dolostone layers of the Lockport with mineralized solution cavities are exposed, specimens may be found. However, four quarries in the west and one ravine in the east have produced the largest number of noteworthy specimens.

Niagara Falls Quarry (43°07'36"N, 78°57'22"W) at 8875 Quarry Road, Niagara, NY, opened in 1946 and closed in 2007. It was operated as the LaFarge Corp. Quarry and, before that, as the Niagara Redlands Quarry and the Niagara Stone Quarry. Note that it is not actually in the city of Niagara Falls, but rather in the town and county of Niagara.

Lockport Quarry (43°09'17"N, 78°43'17"W) along Hinman Road southwest of Lockport, NY, opened in 1927 and is currently operated as the LaFarge Corp. Quarry. Before that it was operated as the Frontier Dolomite Products Quarry.

Penfield Quarry (43°08'44"N, 77°28'49"W) along Whalen Road near Penfield, NY, opened in 1928 and is currently operated as the Dolomite Products Co., Inc. Quarry.

Walworth Quarry (43°10'06"N, 77°19'04"W) at 4800 Atlantic Avenue in Walworth, NY, was opened in 1962 and is currently operated by Oldcastle Materials, Inc. of Ireland. Previously it was operated as the Dolomite Products Co., Inc. Quarry.

Root Glen (43°02'54"N, 75°24'18"W) is a natural ravine on the campus of Hamilton College in Clinton, NY, that exposes Lockport dolostone partway down the hill.

The mineralization in cavities in the Lockport Group was noticed early in the nineteenth century. In 1808, American mineralogist Archibald Bruce published a report of fluorite (fluate of lime) from rocks near Niagara Falls, which he believed was the first report of this mineral in the United States. In 1824, Amos Eaton published an account of the geological and agricultural aspects of the land along the Erie Canal. He summarized the mineralization in the Lockport Group, then known as the "secondary geodiferous lime," as being prominently exposed both at Niagara Falls and at Lockport. About the exposure at Niagara Falls, he wrote:

> Its thickness upwards extends to the top of the falls, and considerably higher in some places. Here it presents its geodiferous character in a pre-eminent degree. In the geodes we find snowy gypsum, selenite, dogtooth spar, pearl spar, fluor spar, waxy zinc blende, sulphate of strontian, and quartz crystals. (Eaton 1824, 132)

Fig. 31. *Sphalerite. Niagara Falls Quarry, Niagara Co. 3 cm. New York State Museum. GBG*

Note that modern mineral names had not yet been universally adopted, so that Eaton's list of minerals would now read gypsum, calcite, dolomite, fluorite, sphalerite, celestine, and quartz.

The twentieth century saw the opening of large quarries in the western portions of the Lockport dolostones for both rip rap and crushed stone. Thereafter, many thousands of specimens were preserved by mineral collectors. Although many individuals collected noteworthy specimens, particularly fine suites of Lockport minerals from the Niagara Falls and Lockport quarries were assembled by George Medakovich and James Ahl of the Buffalo area. In the Rochester area, two brothers, Charles and Robert Hiler, collected and preserved many significant specimens from the Penfield Quarry. Adrian La Buz of New Hartford collected many impressive specimens of sphalerite from Root Glen and other ravines that expose the Lockport in its eastern range.

Fig. 32. *Fluorite. Penfield Quarry, Penfield, Monroe Co. 5 cm crystal. New York State Museum. GBG*

Geology and Origin

The several separately named layers of the Lockport Group formed at shallow depths in a moderately warm, inland marine environment about 420 million years ago (Middle Silurian). Like most dolostones, these originally formed as limestones and were later converted to dolostones. As the seas dried up, anhydrite concretions formed in some layers and were subsequently dissolved away producing solution cavities conducive to mineralization.

Fluid-inclusion studies of Lockport fluorite have yielded temperatures of formation between 150° and 170° C leading to the conclusion that mineralization of the cavities occurred during burial by overlying sediments as thick as three miles. The mineralizing solutions appear to have been three to seven times more saline than seawater and were enriched in the elements characteristic of the minerals that were deposited. Both the Alleghenian Orogeny (250 to 200 million years ago) and the Acadian Orogeny (400 to 325 million years ago) have been suggested as periods that would have mobilized mineralizing fluids. Subsequently, erosion exposed the mineralized layers at the surface.

Minerals

A significant number of mineral species have been described from various exposures of the Lockport dolostones. Of these, aragonite, barite, chalcopyrite, hematite, pyrite, smithsonite, strontianite, sulfur, and witherite are of rare occurrence or generally not of sufficient quality to be of particular interest to mineral collectors. The species listed below, however, have been found as excellent specimens.

Anhydrite, $CaSO_4$, is relatively common at the westernmost exposures of the Lockport. Most often the original anhydrite nodules may still contain some anhydrite, but are largely altered to granular white gypsum. More rarely, unaltered lavender pinacoidal crystals in groups to 5 cm have been found at Lockport.

Calcite, $CaCO_3$, is ubiquitous in cavities at all exposures of the Lockport dolostones. Most commonly, calcite crystals form untwinned scalenohedra that range from white to ivory to yellow in color. Individual crystals larger than several centimeters are uncommon.

Celestine, $SrSO_4$, occurs as tabular or prismatic crystals to 20 cm. Many are transparent to translucent and range from colorless to white, pale blue, and pale honey brown. While celestine may be found throughout the Lockport, the Penfield quarry has traditionally produced many of the larger, higher-quality specimens.

Dolomite, $CaMg(CO_3)_2$, is common at the four quarries as ivory to pink saddle-shaped crystals to a centimeter or more lining cavities. The fossils occasionally found in cavities with the various crystallized minerals are usually replaced by dolomite and quartz. In eastern exposures near Cicero, NY, dolomite occurs as simple, transparent, colorless to amber rhombohedra to 4 cm.

Fluorite, CaF_2, is most common at the Penfield and Walworth quarries. At Penfield, cubes as large as 8 cm are encountered. Some have a frosted surface, while others are glassy and transparent. Crystals that are blue in sunlight and gray in artificial light are occasionally found. Colorless, yellow, and purple crystals are common and often display dramatic color zoning. At Walworth, most fluorite crystals are glassy, transparent, pale blue cubes, often with stepped faces. Most of these are smaller than 3 cm. Dark purple cubic crystals are also sometimes found. At the Niagara Falls quarry, fluorite is less common and occurs as dark purple glassy cubes. Fluorite is uncommon at the Lockport quarry, but sometimes shows interesting green zones at the corners of otherwise colorless to gray cubic crystals.

Galena, PbS, occurs as metallic gray crystals with dull to shiny luster. Cubes and cubes with octahedral faces are most common. Usually, galena crystals are only several millimeters, but splendent crystals to 2 cm have occasionally been found in exposures near Chadwicks, NY, and cubes to 4 cm, but with a duller luster, have been found at the Penfield and Walworth quarries. Cubo-octahedral crystals to 1 cm occur at the Lockport quarry.

Gypsum, $CaSO_4·2H_2O$, is a common mineral at all four quarries, forming white granular replacement textures of original anhydrite concretions, but also partially filling cavities with sheets of transparent colorless selenite as the last mineral to form. Cleavages, often with other crystals along one edge to 10 cm or more, are relatively common, and very large plates to 70 cm or more are occasionally encountered. Euhedral crystals of gypsum are much less common, but have been found at the Penfield quarry in terminated crystals to 15 cm or more, sometimes in arrays of parallel crystals.

Marcasite, FeS_2, is a common mineral at many exposures, usually forming acicular silvery to brassy crystals on dolomite crystals or embedded in transparent gypsum. Repeated twinning sometimes produces reticulated arrays of crystals.

Quartz, SiO_2, is commonly seen replacing fossils in the four quarries but is uncommon as crystals. By contrast, in Root Glen, it forms sharp colorless prismatic crystals to 1 cm, often with white scalenohedral calcite crystals to several centimeters.

Sphalerite, ZnS, occurs almost everywhere mineralized cavities are encountered in the Lockport dolostone, and shows a wide range of crystal habits and colors. At the Niagara Falls quarry, sphalerite tends to be red to reddish brown and occurs as clusters of almost tabular crystals with curved faces. At the Lockport quarry, a characteristic habit consists of millimeter-sized yellow to orange-yellow crystals that form spherical starbursts to 1 cm or more, though very lustrous equant black crystals to 5 mm are also occasionally encountered. Sphalerite crystals at the Penfield quarry tend to be equant, rather than tabular, and are often brown to reddish brown, occasionally altered on the surface to dull creamy white to yellow smithsonite. Sphalerite crystals at Penfield form clusters that sometimes exceed 3 or 4 cm across. At the Walworth quarry, sphalerite tends to occur in flattened clusters of oriented reddish to reddish brown crystals to 3 cm, as well as yellow, orange, and almost black equant crystals to 1 cm. Crystals from Root Glen in the eastern part of the exposure, however, are the largest and have the sharpest crystal faces. Dark reddish brown crystals to several centimeters with high luster, flat faces, and good transparency occur in cavities with colorless quartz crystals, white calcite crystals, and small bisphenoids of chalcopyrite.

Similar Occurrences

Street excavations in Chili, northwest of Rochester, and Cicero, when I-81 was built (43°10'32"N, 76°06'57"W); Whiting quarry in North Syracuse (43°10'49"N, 76°04'21"W); exposures along Oneida Lake near Bridgeport (43°09'44"N, 75°55'37"W); exposures along Rt. 5 near Lairdsville (43°04'22"N, 75°30'06"W); and exposures near Chadwicks (43°01'50"N, 75°16'44"W). Any construction project that exposes the Lockport should be investigated for possible mineralization.

Fig. 34. Celestine. Penfield Quarry, Penfield, Monroe Co. 9 cm. Steven C. Chamberlain collection. SCC

Fig. 33. Calcite, dolomite. Penfield Quarry, Penfield, Monroe Co. 8 cm. Steven C. Chamberlain collection. MW

Fig. 35. Marcasite, gypsum. Penfield Quarry, Penfield, Monroe Co. 4 mm. Steven C. Chamberlain collection. SCC

Fig. 36. *Fluorite, dolomite. Penfield Quarry, Penfield, Monroe Co. 6 cm. New York State Museum. GBG*

Fig. 38. *Fluorite. Walworth Quarry, Walworth, Wayne Co. 5 cm crystal. New York State Museum. MH*

Fig. 37. *Sphalerite, calcite. Root Glen, Clinton, Madison Co. 6 cm. Steven C. Chamberlain collection. SCC*

Fig. 39. *Fluorite. Walworth Quarry, Walworth, Wayne Co. 4.2 cm. New York State Museum. GBG*

References

AWALD, C. J. (1958) Minerals of the Niagara frontier region. *Science on the March* 38:98-107.

AWALD, C. J. (1969) Minerals of the Niagara frontier region. *Science on the March* 49:48-51, 57-59.

BAILEY, D. G., HAWKINS, M., and HILER, C. (2009) Minerals of the Silurian Lockport Group, central and western New York State. *Rocks & Minerals* 84:326-337.

BRUCE, A. (1808) Notices concerning fluate of lime and oxide of manganese discovered in the state of New-York. *The Medical Repository* 11:441-442.

DIETRICH, R. V. (1994) What is the Niagara Escarpment? *Rocks & Minerals* 69:191-195.

DOSSERT, W. P., and CHAMBERLAIN, S. C. (1989) A new occurrence of barite in the Lockport Formation in Madison County, New York. *Rocks & Minerals* 64:469-470.

DUNN, A. (1985) The color of sphalerite from the Lockport Dolomite: Relationship to chemical impurities. *Rocks & Minerals* 60:286-287.

EATON, A. (1824) *Geological and Agricultural Survey of the District Adjoining the Erie Canal, in the State of New-York. Part I. Containing a Description of the Rock Formations.* Packard & Van Benthuysen, Albany. 163p.

FRIEDMAN, G. M. (1989) Case history of deep-burial sulfide mineralization in the northern Appalachian Basin. *Carbonates and Evaporites* 4:231-242.

HAWKINS, A. C. (1925) Fluorite from Rochester, New York. *American Mineralogist* 10:34-36.

HAYNES, S. J., and MOSTAGHEL, M. A. (1979) Formation temperature of fluorite in the Lockport Dolomite in upper New York State as indicated by fluid inclusion studies: With discussion of heat sources. *Economic Geology and the Bulletin of the Society of Economic Geologists* 74:154-159.

JENSEN, D. E. (1942) Minerals of the Lockport Dolomite in the vicinity of Rochester, New York. *Rocks & Minerals* 17:199-203.

KINSLAND, G. L. (1977) Formation temperature of fluorite in the Lockport Dolomite in upper New York State as indicated by fluid inclusion studies: With a discussion of heat sources. *Economic Geology and the Bulletin of the Society of Economic Geologists* 72:849-854.

LABUZ, A. (1968) Sphalerite-galena occurrences of central New York State. *Rocks & Minerals* 43:323-328.

MCELWEE, M. A. (1999) Minerals of the Lockport Formation. *Rocks & Minerals* 74:185-186.

MCELWEE, M. A. (2000) Penfield quarry, Monroe County, New York, and Walworth quarry, Wayne County, New York: Past and Present. *Rocks & Minerals* 75:254-255.

MONAHAN, J. W. (1928) Minerals in eastern exposures of the Lockport in New York State. *American Mineralogist* 13:70-71.

WALTER, M. (2007) *Field Collecting Minerals in the Empire State.* Privately published. 212p.

ZENGER, D. H. (1965) Stratigraphy of the Lockport Formation (Middle Silurian) in New York State. *Bulletin of the New York State Museum* 404:1-210.

Chittenango Falls Celestine Occurrence

Significance

The transparent blue celestine crystals from an exposure of the Rondout Formation just north of Chittenango Falls rank among the finest in the world. A number of different strata are mineralized at the occurrence, each producing celestine crystals with different crystal habits and appearance.

Location and History

High cliffs along the east side of NYS Rt. 13 (42°59'12"N, 75°50'44"W), just north of Chittenango Falls in the town of Fenner in Madison County contain celestine and calcite mineralization. Originally, the road between Chittenango and Cazenovia ran on the west side of the stream and the present exposure formed the east wall of a quarry. When the road was moved to the east side of the stream, the abandoned quarry became a road cut.

Some of the first noteworthy celestine specimens were collected from this locality early in the twentieth century by Adam Geer, a mineral collector who lived in Utica, NY. His collection was acquired by the New York State Museum in 1974, a year after his death. In the mid-twentieth century, Adrian Labuz of New Hartford, NY, was a frequent and very successful collector at the site. In the 1980s, William Dossert of Onondaga Hill, NY, collected numerous high-quality specimens. Due to the danger imposed by loose and falling rock, the site is presently closed to collecting and posted by New York State.

Geology and Origin

A dozen or more layers of the Chrysler Member of the upper-Silurian Rondout Formation exposed on the cliffs at this locality are mineralized with various forms and habits of crystallized celestine and calcite. Except for nearby exposures on the former Oscar Olson farm, these strata do not contain celestine at other places where they are exposed in the region, so that the concentration of strontium mineralization appears to be geographically restricted.

Fig. 40. Celestine. Chittenango Falls, Madison Co. 7 cm. Steven C. Chamberlain collection. SCC

In some strata, the mineralization is restricted to a particular horizon and is essentially continuous over distances of many meters. In other strata, the celestine and calcite occur in cavities in concretionary or geodic masses to 10 or 15 centimeters that readily separate intact from the enclosing rock. In still other strata, large, irregular pockets to a meter across occur at various horizons and may be spaced several meters or more apart. No systematic investigation of the relationships between strata and mineralization has ever been published owing, no doubt, to the difficulty in safely accessing mineralization high on the cliffs.

Minerals

Only four minerals have been found at this locality— celestine, calcite, and, very rarely, strontianite and sulfur. Of these, only the first three form specimens of interest to collectors.

Calcite, $CaCO_3$, occurs most commonly as transparent to translucent, colorless to amber colored untwinned scalenohedra to 4 cm. Occasionally colorless to white nailhead habit crystals are also encountered. There is some correlation between the habit of calcite crystals and the habit of associated celestine. Blocky, equant celestine crystals are most often found in pockets with calcite of nailhead habit; whereas transparent, flawless, gemmy, prismatic celestine usually occurs with calcite scalenohedra.

Celestine, $SrSO_4$, occurs in a bewildering array of forms and habits. Thibault studied the crystallography of one of the habits and reported the following forms: pinacoids, $b\{010\}$, $c\{001\}$; prisms, $o\{011\}$, $m\{110\}$, $d\{102\}$, $l\{104\}$, $\Phi\{106\}$, $g\{103\}$, $\Delta_1\{109\}$, $\Sigma\{1.0.11\}$, $\{3.0.29\}$, $\{3.0.31\}$; bipyramids, $z\{111\}$, $\sigma\{221\}$, $y\{122\}$, $v\{324\}$. Most crystals are pale to dark blue, but some are white or colorless. Tabular crystals, often diamond-shaped, are common, as are blocky prismatic crystals. Equant crystals sometimes reach 6 cm in maximum dimension. Some elongated prismatic crystals are zoned with transparent, blue centers and an opaque, white selective overgrowth. Other crystals are flattened, elongated blades with pointed terminations like picket fences. Occasionally, the blue color has a greenish tint, probably because of included microscopic yellow sulfur. A particularly unusual form of celestine is found in seams about 1 cm thick that are concordant with the strata and filled with blue celestine fibers oriented perpendicular to the seam, somewhat resembling the "satin spar" variety of gypsum.

Strontianite, $SrCO_3$, is rare and only a few confirmed specimens are known. Acicular white crystals form hemispherical masses to 1 cm associated with calcite and celestine.

Similar Occurrences

This celestine occurrence, along with the adjacent exposure on the former Oscar Olson farm on top of the cliff is unique in New York State. Celestine also occurs fairly commonly in cavities in the Lockport dolostone across the state, but the color, forms, and associations are quite different.

References

THIBAULT, N. W. (1935) Celestite from Chittenango Falls, New York. *American Mineralogist* 20:147-152.

Fig. 41. Celestine. Chittenango Falls, Madison Co. 7 cm. Steven C. Chamberlain collection. SCC

Fig. 42. Celestine. Chittenango Falls, Madison Co. 5 cm crystal. Steven C. Chamberlain collection. SCC

Fig. 43. Celestine, calcite. Chittenango Falls, Madison Co. 7 cm. Steven C. Chamberlain collection. SCC

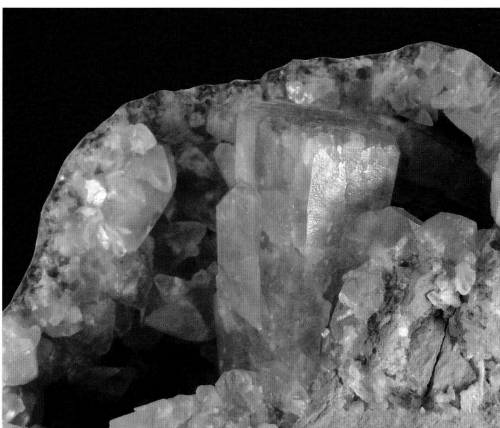

Alden Pyritized Fossil Locality

Significance

This locality is a good example of diagenetic mineralization as a sedimentary rock formed rather than subsequent mineralization of solution cavities. The exposures along Spring Creek in Alden have yielded many excellent specimens of pyritized fossils and are representative of a significant number of such localities in New York State.

Location and History

Spring Creek exposes the Alden Pyrite Bed along its banks (42°54'15"N, 78°29'11"W) between Crittenden Road and US Route 20 in Alden, Erie County, NY.

The locality has been frequented by both mineral and fossil collectors for more than 50 years. It remains an active collecting site and is popular with New York State fossil and mineral clubs.

Geology and Origin

Pyrite concretions, fully or partially enclosing pyritized fossils, occur in a particular layer, the Alden Pyrite Bed, in the Middle Devonian Ledyard Shale Member of the Ludlowville Formation. This bed extends from exposures on the banks of Cazenovia Creek (42°50'08"N, 78°46'28"W) near Aurora, in the west to the banks of Jaycox Creek (42°49'54"N, 77°47'53"W) near Geneseo in the east, and includes exposures on the banks of Elevenmile Creek (42°55'13"N, 78°25'26"W), Murder Creek (42°55'10"N, 78°21'17"W), and an abandoned clay pit west of Bethany Center Road (42°54'57"N, 78°07'59"W), among others.

Often, precipitation of pyrite in shales results from sulfate reduction during burial under low oxygen concentrations. In the case of pyrite concretions intimately associated with fossil remains, such as those in the Alden Pyrite Bed, the reservoir of sulfide to produce pyrite may have come from the breakdown of the organic remains and may have been mediated by biofilms of bacteria, resulting in particularly detailed preservation of biological structures in the resulting pyritized fossil.

The presence of a regional pyrite bed would appear to be the result of the coincidence, for a period of geological time, of low oxygen conditions, a ready source of reactive iron, an abundance of living organisms to be fossilized, and an appropriate burial rate to permit pyritization to proceed. In the Alden Pyrite Bed, brachiopods, bryozoa, corals, crinoids, cephalopods (*Tornoceras uniangulare*), and trilobites (*Phacops rana* and *Greenops boothi*) are all present and well preserved.

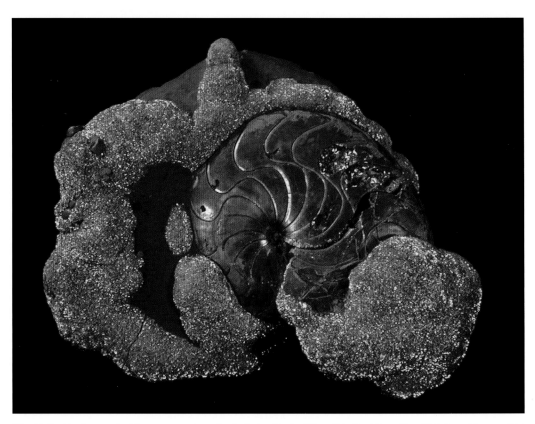

Fig. 44. *Pyritized ammonite* (Tornoceras uniangulare). *Spring Creek, Alden, Erie Co. 6.7 cm. New York State Museum. RB*

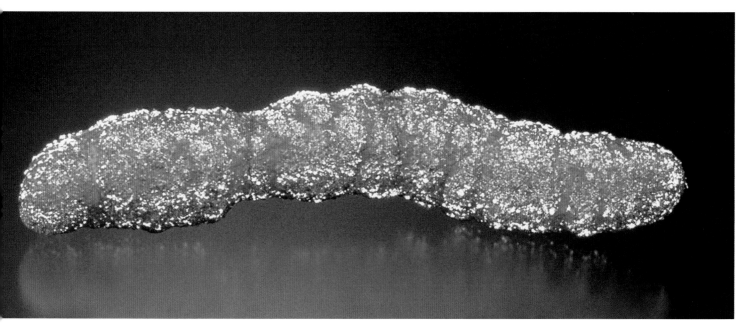

Fig. 45. Pyrite. Spring Creek, Alden, Erie Co. 11 cm. New York State Museum. JAS

Minerals

This is a single mineral locality—pyrite. Earlier reports that the Alden Pyrite Bed contained marcasite have repeatedly been shown to have been in error.

Pyrite, FeS_2, occurs as concretions usually not larger than about 2 cm, but occasionally as large as 7 or 8 cm and rarely even larger. The concretions have minute crystal faces on the surface characteristic of pyrite. The surface of exposed fossils is often very shiny. It is interesting to note that when a pyritized trilobite is removed from its enclosing concretion, the biconvex, single-crystal calcite lenslets in the compound eye are intact, indicating that pyritization did not occur under acidic conditions.

Similar Occurrences

Tully pyritized fossil locality (42°47'59"N, 76°07'16"W); Black River pyritized fossil locality (44°01'00"N, 75°46'38"W).

References

BORKOW, P. S. and BABCOCK, L. E. (2003) Turning pyrite concretions outside-in: Role of biofilms in pyritization of fossils. *The Sedimentary Record* 1(3):4-7.
IZARD, J. E. and CLEMENCY, C. V. (1967) X-ray study of the sedimentary pyrite of western New York. *Journal of Sedimentary Research* 37:221-225.
KENNY, D. (2011) Devonian Alden Pyrite Beds in Western New York. <http://donaldkenney.110mb.com/SITES/NYALDENPYRITE/NYALDENPYRITE.HTM>
LEVI-SETTI, R. (1993) *Trilobite*. 2nd edition. University of Chicago Press, Chicago. 213p.

Ilion Travertine Locality

Significance

This locality is a good example of a mineralizing process in action in a sedimentary rock. Although all the stalactites, stalagmites, and flowstone from this locality are the travertine variety of calcite, their forms have impressive variety.

Location and History

There may be numerous sites along the Ilion Gorge southwest of the city of Ilion, New York, where similar specimens of calcite can be collected, but a particularly productive locality is along Jerusalem Hill Road (42°57'48"N, 75°06'42"W) which runs up the center of Beckus Gulf, north of Cedarville in the Town of Litchfield, Herkimer County, New York.

Excellent specimens of dark brown botryoidal calcite were collected in the 1960s by Adrian La Buz. In the past decade, Bill and Viki Hladysz and Michael Walter collected many specimens of very diverse habit. The site is also a favorite field trip destination for New York mineral clubs.

Geology and Origin

The travertine mineralization lines the sides of a ravine where a stream has exposed layers of Upper Silurian shale. The mechanism by which it forms is the same as that which forms similar material that decorates underground limestone caverns. Groundwater from the soil zone becomes charged with carbon dioxide, forming carbonic acid. As it descends downward through fractures, it dissolves any calcite present in limestones and limy shales. When it exits fractures into an underground chamber, or in this case the edge of a ravine, it releases carbon dioxide and precipitates calcite. This process in ongoing, but intermittent, depending on rainfall and the efficiency with which the plants of the soil zone can charge the ground water that passes downward through it with carbon dioxide. External mineralization occurs when downward percolating groundwater encounters an impermeable layer such as a shale that acts as a confining bed and causes the water to flow laterally and out the sides of a ravine where the travertine variety of calcite is precipitated.

The formation of travertine at this locality is ongoing, and results in a variety of physical forms depending on the local details of how the shale has fallen to produce spaces of various sizes and shapes. One interesting form results when a tree falls down into the ravine and is slowly covered with layers upon layers of travertine. Eventually the wood decomposes and the mineralization proceeds on both the outside and the inside, forming a straight travertine "pipe" that can be tens of feet long.

Minerals

Only layered calcite (travertine) has been found at this locality, but in stalactites, stalagmites, and flowstone.

Calcite, $CaCO_3$, forms layered travertine with layers ranging in thickness from several millimeters to several centimeters and, in color, from creamy white to dark "root beer" brown. Stalactites and stalagmites to 50 cm or more have been collected. The surfaces are sometimes coated with dark brown goethite, and the insides of hollow, "soda-straw" stalactites are sometimes black. Whether the various colors of calcite layers are due to variation in iron content or organic impurities or both has not been investigated.

Similar Occurrences

Ravines near Camillus (43°01'58"N, 76°19'00"W); Howe Caverns (42°41'41"N, 74°23'59"W).

References

WALTER, M. (2004) Travertine from Ilion Gorge. *Rock & Gem* 34(11):88-91.

WALTER, M. (2007) *Field Collecting Minerals in the Empire State*. Privately published. 212p.

Fig. 46. Calcite. Ilion Gorge, Herkimer Co. 9.2 cm. New York State Museum. GBG

Fig. 48. Calcite. Jerusalem Hill, Herkimer Co. 15.8 cm. Steven C. Chamberlain collection. MW

Fig. 47. Calcite. Jerusalem Hill, Herkimer Co. 11.4 cm. Steven C. Chamberlain collection. MW

Fig. 49. Calcite. Jerusalem Hill, Herkimer Co. 9.2 cm. Michael Walter collection. MW

Chapter 3
Occurrences in Crystalline Rocks

This chapter presents detailed accounts of twelve occurrences hosted in crystalline rocks: three in granitic pegmatites and nine in Precambrian metamorphic rocks. Some are historically important localities that are no longer available for collecting: the Bedford pegmatites, the Greenfield chrysoberyl locality, the Overlook quarry, and the Tilly Foster iron mine. The rest are localities that are still available for collecting: the Pierrepont black tourmaline locality, the Bush farm brown tourmaline occurrence, the Natural Bridge titanite occurrence, the Rose Road wollastonite occurrence, the Russell danburite occurrence, the De Kalb gem diopside locality, the West Pierrepont tremolite occurrence, and the Amity-Edenville area in Orange County.

Tilly Foster Iron Mine

Significance

This classic locality is famous for producing large, cinnamon red crystals of chondrodite—among the finest in the world. The crystals of dark green clinochlore, orange-yellow titanite, creamy white brucite, and black magnetite are also of high quality and much sought after by collectors. Numerous pseudomorphs of serpentine after crystals of various minerals are also noteworthy.

Location and History

The Tilly Foster Iron Mine is now a water-filled open pit at (41°24'45"N, 73°38'32"W) on the edge of the Middle Branch Reservoir, northwest of the village of Brewster in the Town of Southeast, Putnam County.

Mining at the iron deposit on the land of Herman King was begun by James E. Townsend in 1810 to supply his nearby forge. Initially, surface excavation of the outcropping ore was sufficient. In 1815, the land was purchased by George Beale, and in 1830, by Tillingham (Tilly) Foster, who owned it for twelve years until he died. During this time, the Townsend family continued mining to supply their forge.

Fig. 50. Chondrodite. Tilly Foster Mine, Brewster, Putnam Co. 5 cm. New York State Museum. SN

Fig. 51. Chondrodite. Tilly Foster Mine, Brewster, Putnam Co. 5 cm. New York State Museum. SN

William W. Mather described the deposit as it appeared while Tilly Foster was still alive:

> A body of magnetic oxide of iron occurs on Mr. Tilly Foster's farm, two and a half miles southeast from Putnam court-house. The ore forms a large part of a hill about one hundred yards long, ten to forty feet broad, and elevated twenty to thirty feet above the ground adjoining. Some hundreds, perhaps thousands of tons of ore can be easily procured at this place, without digging below the level of the hill. It is associated with serpentine, with limestone containing brucite, or boltonite [forsterite], and with green mica [probably clinochlore]. (Mather 1843, 560)

Foster's widow, Mary, inherited the deposit, and in 1853, it was sold to Thomas Harvey and Theodosus Secor who mined under the corporate name, Harvey Iron and Steel. The mine was incorporated under the name Tilly Foster Iron Mine in 1860. Subsequent owners kept the name, and the mine operated until 1897. Mining was challenging and alternated between underground and open-pit operations. In 1887, the mine was converted to the largest open-pit mine in the world at that time.

Mining activities were plagued throughout the period of operation by collapses and falling rocks. On November 29, 1895, 100 tons of rock slid into the pit killing thirteen miners. Although the mine reopened after a series of legal proceedings and inspections and operated for another eighteen months, unfavorable economics finally closed the mine in 1897. At its closure, ore was only being produced in small quantities from the deepest level at 600 feet.

During mining, an active network of miners, supervisors, collectors, and mineral dealers assured a continuing flow of specimens. Private collector Elwood P. Hancock assembled an outstanding collection of Tilly Foster minerals by buying them directly from the miners. His collection is now housed at Harvard University. The noted mineral dealer George L. English also procured specimens directly from these sources and advertised sales of suites of minerals from Tilly Foster.

After the mine closed and the open pit became filled with water, specimens could still readily be obtained from the dumps, which remained a popular destination for mineral clubs in the northeast for thirty years. From 1936 to 1942, John N. Trainer assembled an extensive collection of Tilly Foster specimens, which he donated to the New York State Museum in 1949. Starting in 1942, Ronald E. Januzzi collected from the dumps for more than twenty-five years and added many new species to the list of minerals found at the locality. Januzzi's collection has since been dispersed. Around 1970, the owners of the site posted it to prevent mineral collecting, and the remaining dumps have been off limits ever since.

Geology and Origin

The Tilly Foster Iron mine is hosted by Precambrian metamorphic rocks in the Hudson Highlands. The deposit appears to be a magnetite-bearing, mafic-ultramafic intrusion that was subjected to metamorphism by residual igneous fluids.

Minerals

Many of the 100 or so species reported from this locality were recovered from the dumps long after mining stopped. No modern study has endeavored to verify the various species listed here. A working list of mineral species and groups found at the Tilly Foster Iron Mine includes: actinolite, albite, allanite, anglesite, ankerite, apatite, apophyllite, aragonite, arsenopyrite, augite, autunite, axinite, barite, biotite, bornite, brochantite, brucite, calcite, cerussite, chalcopyrite, chondrodite, chrysocolla, clinochlore, clinohumite, danburite, datolite, diopside, dolomite, enstatite, epidote, erythrite, fluorite, galena, garnet, goethite, gold, graphite, gypsum, hedenbergite, hematite, hexahydrite, heulandite, hisingerite, hornblende, humite, hydromagnesite, hydrotalcite, ilmenite, jarosite, kaolin, laumontite, lepidocrocite, linarite, linnaeite, magnesite, magnetite, malachite, marcasite, melanterite, microcline, molybdenite, muscovite, natrolite, olivine, opal, pectolite, phlogopite, posnjakite, prehnite, psilomelane, pyrite, pyrolusite, pyrrhotite, quartz, riebeckite, rutile, scapolite, scheelite, serpentine, serpierite, siderite, spinel, stilbite, sulfur, szomolnokite, talc, thomsonite, thorite, titanite, tourmaline, and tremolite. Of these, only those yielding excellent specimens are described below.

Brucite, $Mg(OH)_2$, occurs as pale blue to creamy white tabular crystals to 2 cm or more in clusters to 10 cm or more.

Chondrodite, $(Mg,Fe)_5(SiO_4)_2(F,OH)_2$, intermixed with magnetite, formed the major portion of the ore. Crystals to 3 cm range in color from pale orange-red to bright cinnamon-red to dark reddish brown to almost black. Many crystals have very lustrous faces, although some are dull and frosted, while others have flawless, transparent areas. The best of these rank with the finest examples of this species found anywhere in the world. Green and brown serpentine pseudomorphs after chondrodite crystals are often very sharply formed, most often with a dull surface luster.

Clinochlore, $(Mg,Al)_6(Si,Al)_4O_{10}(OH)_8$, occurs most commonly as tabular dark green crystals, sometimes with very lustrous edges. Most such crystals are 3 cm or smaller, but a few may approach 5 cm or more across. More rarely, clinochlore occurs as elongated, prismatic, almost black crystals.

Magnetite, Fe_3O_4, formed the iron ore. Splendent, metallic, black, dodecahedral crystals to 3 cm form matrix specimens often with chondrodite and clinochlore. However, most magnetite crystals are smaller and frequently have dull surface luster.

Titanite, $CaTiSiO_5$, occurs as flattened yellow crystals to several centimeters, sometimes tending to orange. Many titanite specimens in collections came from an isolated occurrence encountered in 1891 that produced several hundred specimens of gem-quality crystals. Greenish, brown, and yellow crystals to 1 cm or more are relatively rare.

Pseudomorphs, most commonly serpentine replacements of other minerals, are present in great variety. All are a pale shade of green or pale brown in color and show the crystal form of the original mineral. These include serpentine pseudomorphs after: apatite, calcite, clinochlore, chondrodite, dolomite, and other minerals, some unidentified.

Similar Occurrences

Mahopac mine (41°23'48"N, 73°45'39"W). This occurrence has similar features and overall mineralogy, petrology, and geochemistry, but never produced the spectacular specimens for which Tilly Foster is famous.

Fig. 52. Chondrodite. Tilly Foster Mine, Brewster, Putnam Co. 5 cm. New York State Museum. SN

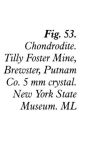

Fig. 53. Chondrodite. Tilly Foster Mine, Brewster, Putnam Co. 5 mm crystal. New York State Museum. ML

Fig. 54. Clinochlore. Tilly Foster Mine, Brewster, Putnam Co. 1.8 cm crystal. Harvard Mineralogical Museum. ML

References

BREIDENBAUGH, E. S. (1873) On the minerals found at the Tilly Foster iron mines, N. Y. *American Journal of Science*, series 3, 6:207-213.

DANA, E. S. (1875a) Preliminary notice of chondrodite crystals from the Tilly Foster mine, Brewster, New York. *American Journal of Science*, series 3, 9:63-64.

DANA, E. S. (1875b) On the chondrodite crystals from the Tilly Foster mine, Brewster, New York. *American Journal of Science*, series 3, 10:89-103.

DANA, J. D. (1874) On serpentine pseudomorphs and other kinds from the Tilly Foster iron mine, Putnam County, New York. *American Journal of Science*, series 3, 8:371-381.

JANUZZI, R. E. (1966) *A Field Mineralogy of the Tilly Foster Iron Mine.* Mineralogical Press. 161p.

JOHNSON, T. (2011) Mineralogy of the Tilly Foster Iron Mine. *Rochester Mineralogical Symposium Program Notes* 38:40-43.

MATHER, W. W. (1843) *Geology of New-York, Part I. Geology of the First Geological District.* Carroll & Cook, Albany, NY. 653p. + plates.

NIGHTINGALE, S. L. (2001) The Tilly Foster Iron Mine: Southeast, Putnam County, New York. *Matrix* 9:51-79.

NUWER, H. (1971) The Tilly Foster mine. *Rocks & Minerals* 46:147-154.

TRAINER, J. N. (1938) Tilly Foster up-to-date. *Rocks & Minerals* 13:291-303.

TRAINER, J. N. (1939) Tilly Foster up-to-date. *Rocks & Minerals* 14:50-52.

TRAINER, J. N. (1940) Another year at Tilly Foster. *Rocks & Minerals* 15:126-128.

TRAINER, J. N. (1941) The fifth year at Tilly Foster. *Rocks & Minerals* 16:122-126.

TRAINER, J. N. (1942) Sixth year at Tilly Foster. *Rocks & Minerals* 17:8-9.

TRAINER, J. N. (1943) More about Tilly Foster. *Rocks & Minerals* 18:168-179.

ZODAC, P. (1938) Some recent finds at Tilly Foster. *Rocks & Minerals* 13:180-181.

Fig. 55. Clinochlore, Magnetite. Tilly Foster Mine, Brewster, Putnam Co. 5 cm fov. A. E. Seaman Mineral Museum. GWR

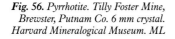

Fig. 56. Pyrrhotite. Tilly Foster Mine, Brewster, Putnam Co. 6 mm crystal. Harvard Mineralogical Museum. ML

Fig. 57. Serpentine pseudomorph after dolomite. Tilly Foster Mine, Brewster, Putnam Co. 5.5 cm crystal. Harvard Mineralogical Museum. ML

Fig. 58. Titanite. Tilly Foster Mine, Brewster, Putnam Co. 7 cm fov. New York State Museum. SN

Amity-Edenville Area, Orange County

Significance

Although Orange County is home to the type localities for five different minerals (warwickite, clintonite, edenite, fluoro-potassichastingsite, and fluoropargasite), it is probably better known to mineral collectors for its large crystals of scapolite, diopside, and spinel, the latter of which have achieved world recognition for their remarkable size and quality.

Location and History

Located only fifty miles northwest of New York City, Orange County was one of the earliest areas to have been explored for minerals and, therefore, has some of the oldest mineral localities in the United States. Most of these are reported in the literature simply as in the vicinities of Amity, Edenville, and Monroe. However, today much of the land in the county is privately owned, and access is restricted. Combined with inadequate documentation, changes in township boundaries and place names, secrecy, and the passage of nearly two centuries, many of these localities unfortunately have been lost to time.

Knowing that large, well-formed crystals of a variety of minerals were to be found there, it is surprising that relatively few collectors appear to have visited these localities, allowing nature to reclaim them one by one. It becomes even more astonishing when one reads contemporary accounts of what collecting spinel crystals near Amity was like as told by Samuel Fowler in 1825:

> ... I made a discovery in the township of Warwick, Orange County, N. Y. of minerals, the most extraordinary for magnitude and beauty, which have ever yet come to notice. What will be thought of *Spinelle pleonaste*, the side of one of whose bases measures three to four inches, or twelve to sixteen inches in circumference? (Fowler 1825, 242)

In 1832, Charles Shepard described another nearby locality for large, brown, octahedral crystals of spinel, noting "a single crystal from this place weighing fifty-nine pounds." In the 1840s, Silas Horton and John Jenkins collected large spinels in secrecy from an undisclosed locality. They exhibited them in 1853 at the Crystal Palace Exhibition in New York City. Afterwards, Horton sold them to the New York State Museum. In the 1960s, good specimens of gray octahedral spinel crystals were collected on the Rudy farm near Edenville (41°16'39"N, 74°25'43"W), and in 2010, Glenn Rhein, a local contractor, fortuitously uncovered some crystal-studded blocks of scapolite-pyroxene gneiss in contact with coarsely crystallized Franklin Marble while excavating for a house. Some of these have pockets 30–60 cm across lined with terminated crystals of scapolite and pyroxene (probably diopside or augite) several centimeters in length. Other pockets of similar proportions have yielded fine specimens of blue-gray fluorapatite crystals, dark brown and black amphibole crystals (probably edenite or pargasite), and brown crystals of titanite. The marble itself contains well-formed crystals of graphite as well as bands of white diopside, fluoro-edenite, and chondrodite that fluoresce blue and yellow in UV light. Gray-black spinel and orange-brown chondrodite crystals were found in a serpentinized marble matrix in a second nearby excavation, proving the area is still capable of producing worthwhile specimens.

Geology and Origin

The minerals of greatest interest to collectors are those found in the Franklin Marble and related contact metamorphic assemblages whose origins may be linked to the Grenville Orogeny in late Precambrian time. Original carbonate sequences interlayered with siliceous beds were transformed into marble and skarn-like assemblages. At some sites, the skarn minerals show evidence of retrograde metamorphism; at others, local igneous intrusions form contact aureoles in the marble about their peripheries that are rich in chondrodite and spinel. These metasedimentary rocks host most of the important collecting sites, and are best exposed in the Amity–Edenville area and in the vicinity of Twin Lakes (formerly Two Ponds) in Monroe. Because these are the localities that have produced the majority of specimens of collector interest, they are the only ones discussed here.

Minerals

The species descriptions that follow are not comprehensive, but rather represent those minerals for which Orange County is most famous. Many of the best specimens of spinel and other minerals seen in museums were found in the first half of the nineteenth century, and their specific localities are now lost. When known, GPS coordinates for localities are given; otherwise, only vague locality information taken from the references that follow can be provided.

Allanite Series, $(Ca,Ce,Y)_2(Al,Fe^{3+}Fe^{2+})_3(SiO_4)_3$ (OH), minerals occur as tabular, black crystals associated with fluorite in pegmatite exposed in an old granite quarry on the NW slope of Mount Adam.

Amphibole Group, $(Na,K)(Ca,Na)_2(Mg,Fe^{2+}Fe^{3+})_5$ $(Si,Al)_8O_{22}(O,OH,F)_2$, minerals occur at sites throughout the county, and include the type localities for edenite, fluoro-potassichastingsite, and fluoropargasite. Lighter colored, gray-white to pale green crystals often embedded in marble are usually called tremolite or actinolite in the older literature, whereas black crystals often associated with dark colored pyroxene and/or scapolite are referred to as "hornblende." However, without a complete chemical analysis it is virtually impossible to determine which species is actually present. A recent investigation of amphiboles from New York in the New York State Museum showed that some of the black crystals are pargasite, and one such crystal labeled only as coming from Edenville, was in fact fluorine-dominant, making it a new mineral species, fluoropargasite. Some of the more prolific amphibole occurrences described in the literature include: edenite as brown, doubly-terminated crystals over 8 cm long with phlogopite in marble just east of Amity; also ~1.2 miles south of Amity; similar crystals with scapolite and pyroxene ~2.5 mile north of Edenville, near the southern base of Mount Eve; also as brown crystals to 10 cm long, 1 mile south of Mount Eve. Good crystals of "hornblende" occur with spinel, chondrodite and graphite "50 rods north of Amity Meeting House" and "in large, perfect crystals" with spinel and other minerals 1 mile southwest of Amity. The type locality for fluoro-potassichastingsite is at the Greenwood mine, just outside the area in Tuxedo

Fig. 59. Clintonite. Amity, Orange Co. 8 cm. New York State Museum. GBG

Fig. 60. Edenite. Edenville, Orange Co. 6 cm.
New York State Museum. GBG

Fig. 61. Spinel, Warwick, Orange Co. 9 cm. New York State Museum. SN

Township. Both fluoro-edenite and fluorotremolite occur at the Atlas Quarry, near Pine Island.

Corundum, Al_2O_3, is not abundant in the Amity–Edenville area, though the few small pink, red, and blue crystals that have been found locally make one wonder if better specimens or perhaps gem-quality material may exist as a yet unfound treasure. Perhaps the most interesting occurrence reported in the literature is given simply as 1 mile southwest of Amity, where white, blue, and reddish crystals occur with spinel in marble.

Chondrodite, $(Mg,Fe^{2+})_5(SiO_4)_2(F,OH)_2$, is a common accessory mineral in the Franklin Marble. It is commonly associated with spinel throughout the area, and locally, the two minerals may form conspicuous orange and black bands 90 cm or more wide in the marble (e.g., at ~0.2 miles southwest of the southern face of Mount Adam). In spite of its abundance, sharp, well-formed crystals of the mineral are rare. Crude crystals measuring 8 x 13 cm and partially altered to serpentine have been found with spinel and phlogopite at the Rudy farm near Edenville (41°16'39"N, 74°25'43"W).

Clintonite, $CaMg_2AlAl_3SiO_{10}(OH)_2$, occurs as bright orange-brown to pinkish-brown micaceous crystals several inches across with spinel in marble on a knoll ~250 yards northeast of Amity crossroads (41°16'13"N, 74°26'56"W).

Graphite, C, is an abundant accessory mineral throughout the Amity area where it is usually seen as fine-grained dark gray bands in the Franklin Marble. Occasionally, however, sharp, tabular, hexagonal crystals occur scattered throughout the marble or attached to pyroxene or other minerals formerly in contact with the marble (e.g., ~250 yards northeast of Amity crossroads).

Ilmenite, $FeTiO_3$, is relatively uncommon in the area, though reasonably good tabular crystals an inch across have been found with spinel in the marble 1 mile southwest of Amity.

Orthoclase, $KAlSi_3O_8$, crystals associated with tourmaline and zircon in gneiss have been reported from Rocky Hill, 3 miles southeast of Warwick.

Pyroxene Group, $(Ca,Na)(Mg,Fe,Al,Ti)(Si,Al)_2O_6$, minerals, like those in the amphibole group, are best identified by chemical analysis. The most common species in Orange County are probably members of the diopside-hedenbergite series, though some augite may also be present. Blocky prismatic black crystals several centimeters in length associated with scapolite crystals of similar proportions have been recently found on the Rhein property. Historically, similar crystals were reported from ~0.4 miles NE of Amity and near Twin Lakes, Woodbury Township (formerly Two Ponds, Monroe Township). Pale brown crystals are reported from the clintonite type locality (q.v.), and in 1887, G. H. Williams described some highly unusual (possibly twinned), yellow-gray diopside crystals with pseudo-hemimorphic symmetry from 2.5 miles north of Edenville.

Rutile, TiO_2, like ilmenite, is relatively uncommon, but is reported two miles west of Amity as small crystals with tourmaline.

Scapolite Group, $(Na,Ca)_4Al_{3-6}Si_{6-9}O_{24}(Cl,CO_3)$, crystals to 15 cm long have been found associated with titanite, pyroxene, and fluorapatite at a number of sites. Among these are the Rhein property near Amity; as large, doubly terminated crystals 0.4 miles northeast of Amity; and in large crystals with pyroxene, titanite, and zircon near Twin Lakes in Woodbury (formerly Two Ponds, Monroe).

Serpentine Group, $Mg_3Si_2O_5(OH)_4$, minerals are common throughout the Franklin Marble, where, together with calcite, they frequently form the matrix for spinel crystal specimens.

Fig. 62. Spinel. Amity, Orange Co. 8.3 cm. New York State Museum. SN

Fig. 63. Spinel. Amity, Orange Co. 17 cm. Steven C. Chamberlain collection. SCC

Fig. 64. Warwickite. Warwick, Orange Co. 5.5 cm. Root collection, New York State Museum. GBG

Serpentine pseudomorphs after olivine and/or chondrodite are also commonly encountered (e.g. at the Rudy Farm [41°16'39"N, 74°25'43"W], near Edenville).

Spinel, $MgAl_2O_4$, is unquestionably the species for which the Amity area has achieved fame as a classic U.S. mineral locality. There are more occurrences reported than can be given here, so only those noted as having produced collector-quality specimens will be listed: crystals in granular marble with serpentine 1 mile southwest of Amity; large, octahedral crystals (one crystal reported as weighing 27 kg!) in marble 0.5 miles southeast of Amity; octahedral crystals with chondrodite, "hornblende," and graphite 50 rods northeast of Amity Meeting House; in large crystals 1 mile south of Amity Meeting House; 1.3 miles southwest of Amity, as pinkish gray octahedrons to 3 cm with serpentine; 2.5 miles north of Edenville, as sharp, lustrous octahedrons to 3 cm; and gray-black octahedrons 3 cm across occur with phlogopite and crude, serpentinized chondrodite crystals at the Rudy Farm (41°16'39"N, 74°25'43"W) near Edenville.

Titanite, $CaTiOSiO_4$, occurs as typically wedge-shaped, brown crystals 2–5 cm across associated with scapolite, pyroxene, dark amphibole crystals, and rarely zircon at several localities in the Amity area. Among the better occurrences are: the Glenn Rhein property near Amity; 0.4 miles northeast of Amity; and near Twin Lakes, Woodbury Township (formerly Two Ponds, Monroe).

Tourmaline Group, $(Na,Ca)(Mg,Fe)_3Al_6BO_3)_3[Si_6O_{18}](OH,O)_4$, minerals most likely in the uvite-dravite-schorl series occur sparingly in a few localities as dark brown glassy crystals associated with edenite and phlogopite (e.g. the Rhein property near Amity) or with orthoclase and zircon in gneiss as at Rocky Hill, 3 miles southeast of Warwick.

Warwickite, $Mg(Ti,Fe^{3+},Al)BO_3O$, is a rare mineral, known from only a few localities worldwide. It was first described by Shepard in 1838, making it one of the first new mineral species to have been found in the United States. Named for the Town of Warwick, warwickite occurs as subhedral brownish black crystals in marble with spinel, forsterite, phlogopite, and other minerals just east of Amity (41°15'57"N, 74°26'22"W).

Zircon, $ZrSiO_4$, occurs rarely as an associate mineral with scapolite, amphibole, and pyroxene. Localities include: the Glenn Rhein property near Amity; 0.4 miles south of Mount Eve; Twin Lakes, Woodbury Township (Two Ponds, Monroe); and with tourmaline and orthoclase in gneiss at Rocky Hill, 3 miles southeast of Warwick.

Similar Occurrences

Hicks farm (44°18'59"N, 75°39'02"W) northwest of Oxbow; Chilson Hill graphite mines near Ticonderoga (43°54'02"N,73°28'10"W); Olmstedville and Minerva Lake scapolite and vesuvianite localities (43°46'31"N, 73°56'34"W; 43°47'20"N, 73°58'24"W); Natural Bridge (Farr property) and Rose Road (Mulvaney) wollastonite localities (44°04'25"N, 75°28'22"W; 44°12'05"N, 75°13'51"W); Scott farm titanite/zircon locality in Fine (44°13'36"N, 75°06'11"W).

References

AGAR, W. M. (1923) Contact metamorphism in the western Adirondacks. *Proceedings of the American Philosophical Society* 62:95-174.

AYERS, V. L. (1945) Mineral localities of Monroe, New York, and Bear Mountain Park. *Rocks and Minerals* 20(10):468-470.

BECK, L. C. (1842) *Mineralogy of New-York.* Thurlow Weed, Printer to the State, Albany, New York.

COSMINSKY, P. R. (1947) A trip to Mt. Adam and Pine Island, Orange County, New York. *Rocks & Minerals* 22(3):207-209.

FOWLER, S. (1825) An account of some new and extraordinary minerals discovered in Warwick, Orange County, New York. *American Journal of Science*, Series 1, 9:242-245.

HORTON, W. (1843) List of minerals observed in making the examination of the County of Orange. In Mather, W. W. (1843) *Natural History of New York, Part IV Geology.* Carroll and Cook, Albany, New York.

KEARNS, L. E. (1978) The Amity area, Orange County, New York. *Mineralogical Record* 9(2):85-90.

LUPULESCU, M. (2008) Amphibole-group minerals from New York State. *Rocks & Minerals* 83:210-219.

LUPULESCU, M. V., RAKOVAN, J., ROBINSON, G.W., and HUGHES, J. M. (2005) Fluoropargasite, a new member of the calcic amphiboles from Edenville, Orange County, New York. *Canadian Mineralogist* 43:1423-1428.

LUPULESCU, M.V., RAKOVAN, J., DARBY DYAR, M., ROBINSON, G.W., and HUGHES, J.M. (2009) Fluoro-potassichastingsite from the Greenwood Mine, Orange County, New York: a new end-member calcic amphibole. *Canadian Mineralogist*, 47:909-916.

NASON, F. L. (1888) Some New York Minerals and Their Localities. *New York State Museum Bulletin No. 4.*

SHEPARD, C. U. (1832) A sketch of the mineralogy and geology of the counties of Orange (N. Y.) and Sussex (N. J.). *American Journal of Science*, Series 1, 21:321-334.

SHEPARD, C. U. (1838) Notice of warwickite, a new mineral species. *American Journal of Science*, Series 1, 34:313-315.

WHITLOCK, H. P. (1903) List of New York Mineral Localities. *New York State Museum Bulletin No. 70.*

WILLIAMS, G. H. (1887) Note on some remarkable crystals of pyroxene from Orange County, N. Y. *American Journal of Science*, Series 3, 34:275-276.

Natural Bridge Titanite Occurrence

Significance

This early classic locality has produced very sharp crystals of titanite, meionite, zircon, diopside, microcline, and wollastonite. The titanite and wollastonite rank among the finest crystals of those species from anywhere in the United States.

Location and History

The locality consists of two parallel trenches at 44°04'25"N, 75°28'22"W, just east of NY Rt. 3 about 2 miles northeast of the village of Natural Bridge in Lewis County. The property is currently owned by the KOA on the other side of Rt. 3.

This locality was first noted before 1840 when Charles Upham Shepard published a description of his visit there to collect titanite:

> I had the pleasure of obtaining from two recently discovered localities, highly perfect crystals of the mineral under consideration. One of these was on Mr. Cleveland's farm, near a place called Natural Bridge, in Lewis county, where it occurs in small quantity, in coarse granular limestone, associated with a dark colored pyroxene, a pearl-blue scapolite (nuttallite), and crystallized white feldspar. (Shepard 1840, 357)

By 1850, Franklin B. Hough had reported that the locality was owned by Enoch Cleveland and added zircon to the list of minerals found there. Subsequently the noted mineral dealer Chester D. Nims collected and sold Natural Bridge specimens worldwide. In 1900, the land was part of the Ashmore farm and in 1948, part of the Whitestone farm. For the past several decades the property has been owned by Bradley G. Farr of Natural Bridge.

Prior to 1975, the majority of specimens had been extracted from the southern vein, and the northern vein had only been excavated at its western end. After 1975, the northern vein was excavated to the east by Steven C. Chamberlain and George W. Robinson, and later by Charles Bowman. In the 1980s, the southern vein was cleared of debris, and more specimens were collected along the bottom by William Dossert and Steven C. Chamberlain where more than 100 years of acid rain had dissolved the calcite core to a still greater depth. In the 1990s, a cross-cutting vein between the northern and southern veins was discovered and excavated by Angus MacPherson and Jeff Paquette.

Geology and Origin

The two veins appear to be skarn assemblages that formed when the syenite of the Diana Complex intruded the Grenville Marble. Subsequently, regional metamorphism changed the syenite into a syenitic gneiss and is probably responsible for the alteration of meionite to prehnite, titanite to "leucoxene" or rutile, wollastonite to hedenbergite, calcite, and quartz, and the formation of ferro-actinolite as a coating on the diopside (uralitization) in the veins. The later alteration of the vein appears to have involved solutions enriched in iron compared to the original skarn minerals. The ferro-actinolite contains significantly more iron than the diopside it coats. Similarly, both the hedenbergite and diopside that replace wollastonite contain significant iron, but the original wollastonite is virtually iron free.

Fig. 65. *Titanite. Natural Bridge, Lewis Co. 10 cm. Harvard Mineralogical Museum. SCC*

Fig. 66. *Wollastonite. Natural Bridge, Lewis Co. 30 cm. Root collection, New York State Museum. SCC*

Minerals

Most of the minerals listed below occur as sharp crystals lining the walls of the veins or isolated within the calcite that fills their centers.

Calcite, $CaCO_3$, fills the cores of the veins enclosing crystallized silicates along both walls. The massive calcite is gray-green in color and coarsely crystallized, producing cleavage rhombohedra to 5 cm.

Diopside, $CaMgSi_2O_6$, occurs as lustrous dark green to almost black prismatic crystals to 10 cm. Frequently they have a thin coating of dull bluish white ferro-actinolite. Both the lateral pinacoids, $a\{100\}$ and $b\{010\}$ along with the prism $m\{110\}$ form the prismatic zone with terminations commonly formed by $u\{111\}$, often showing only two faces per termination. Occasionally the terminations consist of $u\{111\}$, $o\{\bar{2}21\}$, $s\{\bar{1}11\}$ and $p\{\bar{1}01\}$. Rarely, diopside crystals show twinning with contact plane (100) and terminal faces of the forms $o\{\bar{2}21\}$, $s\{\bar{1}11\}$ and $z\{021\}$.

Ferro-actinolite, $Ca_2Fe_5Si_8O_{22}(OH)_2$, probably represents uralitization and forms dull bluish white coatings on some diopside crystals.

Fluorapatite, $Ca_5(PO_4)_3F$, is uncommon as green crystals to several centimeters. Usually it is found as transparent green crystals to 2 mm in calcite.

Hedenbergite, $CaFeSi_2O_6$, is one of the species that replaces wollastonite, along with quartz, diopside, and calcite.

Meionite, $Ca_4Al_6Si_6O_{24}CO_3$, occurs as blue-green ("nuttalite"), gray, and white, well-formed crystals to 8 cm or more. Crystals are usually equant rather than prismatic and show equal development of forms $a\{100\}$, $m\{110\}$, and $r\{111\}$. The forms $c\{001\}$, $z\{311\}$ and $z_1\{131\}$ are often present as smaller faces. Chemically, the scapolite is close to end-member meionite with a Ca:Na ratio of 16:1.

Microcline, $KAlSi_3O_8$, forms white to translucent gray crystals to several centimeters. Rarely, Baveno twins on $\{021\}$ occur. In thin sections, crystals show a cryptoperthitic texture with minor albite.

Prehnite, $Ca_2Al_2Si_3O_{10}(OH)_2$, can be observed in thin sections as a white alteration product of meionite.

Quartz, SiO_2, in anhedral grains, occurs as one of the alteration products of wollastonite.

Rutile, TiO_2, uncommonly occurs as dark red prismatic crystals to 1 mm that formed as an alteration product of titanite.

Titanite, $CaTiSiO_5$, forms dark brown to black, splendent crystals to 7 cm on edge. Two crystal habits are common: one with prominent development of the three forms, $n\{111\}$, $m\{1\bar{1}0\}$, and $c\{001\}$, and the other with the fourth form $t\{\bar{1}11\}$. The second habit is the variety "lederite" originally described from the locality by C. U. Shepard. The sharp, lustrous crystals of titanite have made this locality famous. Some titanite crystals are altered to a dull white to tan material, often referred to as "leucoxene." At other localities leucoxene is usually made up of grains of anatase and/or rutile; however, at this locality, the alteration product is an amorphous titanium oxide with rare euhedral microcrystals of rutile dispersed throughout.

Wollastonite, $CaSiO_3$, is common and forms prismatic crystals to 30 cm. Most wollastonite crystals, however, are wholly or partially altered. Unaltered wollastonite crystals do occur tightly embedded in calcite. Altered crystals are a mixture of quartz and calcite domains interspersed with long acicular crystals of hedenbergite aligned along the c-axis of the original wollastonite. Irregular partitions cutting across the c-axis are diopside.

Zircon, $ZrSiO_4$, occurs as sharp prismatic crystals to 2 cm, but most are smaller. Larger crystals are pinkish brown and translucent; smaller crystals are honey brown and transparent. Three crystal forms are typically present; prominent $m\{110\}$, $p\{111\}$, and $u\{331\}$ faces, typically unequally developed.

Similar Occurrences

Rose Road wollastonite occurrence (44°12'05"N, 75°13'51"W); Minerva Lake (near 43°47'20"N, 73°58'24"W).

References

BECK, L. C. (1842) *Mineralogy of New-York*. W. & A. White and J. Visscher, Albany. 536p.

BOHLEN, S. R., VALLEY, J. W., and ESSENE, E. J. (1985) Metamorphism in the Adirondacks: I. Petrology, pressure, and temperature. *Journal of Petrology* 26:971-992.

CHAMBERLAIN, S. C. (1985) New occurrences of twinned crystals in St. Lawrence and Lewis Counties, New York. *Rocks & Minerals* 60:285-286.

CHAMBERLAIN, S. C., KING, V. T., COOKE, D., ROBINSON, G. W., and HOLT, W. (1999) Minerals of the Gouverneur Talc Company No. 4 Quarry (Valentine Deposit), Town of Diana, Lewis County, New York. *Rocks & Minerals* 74:236-249.

CHAMBERLAIN, S. C., ROBINSON, G. W., and SMITH, C. A. (1987) The occurrence of wollastonite and titanite, Natural Bridge, Lewis County, New York. *Rocks & Minerals* 62:78-89.

GERDES, M. L., and VALLEY, J. W. (1994) Fluid flow and mass transport at the Valentine wollastonite deposit, Adirondack Mountains, New York State. *Journal of Metamorphic Geology* 12:589-608.

HOUGH, F. B. (1847) Observations on the geology of Lewis County. *American Journal of Agriculture and Science* 5:267-274.

HOUGH, F. B. (1848) Mineral localities in New York. *American Journal of Science*, Series 2 5:132-133.

ROBINSON, G. and CHAMBERLAIN, S. C. (1985) Mineralogy of the titanite occurrence near Natural Bridge, New York. *Rocks & Minerals* 60:288-289.

SHEPARD, C. U. (1840) On a supposed new mineral species. *American Journal of Science* 39:357-360.

SLOCUM, H. W. (1948) Rambles in a collector's paradise, Part 2. *Rocks & Minerals* 23:579-589.

VALLEY, J. W., BOHLEN, S. R., ESSENE, E. J., and LAMB, W. (1990) Metamorphism in the Adirondacks: II. The role of fluids. *Journal of Petrology* 31:555-596.

Rose Road Wollastonite Occurrence near Pitcairn

Significance

This classic locality has produced excellent crystals of wollastonite, titanite, diopside, albite, and fluorapatite, as well as several different pseudomorphs after wollastonite. It is one of only three localities in New York State for good crystals of wollastonite and is the source of some of the finest titanite crystals found anywhere in the state. It has been a productive locality for more than a century and is likely to remain so into the future.

Location and History

The locality occupies the southern end of a ridge that extends southward from Rose Road near its intersection with Rt. 3 at 44°12'05"N, 75°13'51"W in the Town of Pitcairn. At present, it is a fee locality open to the public.

This occurrence appears to have been discovered sometime after the Civil War, and by the 1880s mention of specimens from the locality entered the published literature. During this time, noted mineral collector and dealer Chester D. Nims of Philadelphia, NY, was collecting and marketing specimens from the locality. In the past fifty years, the locality was successively known as the MacDonald sugar bush, the Mulvaney property, the Wade property, the LaPlatney property, and the Rose Road occurrence. Richard LaPlatney, Jr. is the current owner.

Mention of titanite, pyroxene, feldspar, and the crystal forms of wollastonite from the locality were all published in the interval 1885 to 1896. Although some collecting was probably done in the early twentieth century, interest heightened in the second half of the century and important specimens were collected in the 1970s and 1980s by Ronald Waddell, William S. Condon, Steven C. Chamberlain, George W. Robinson, and Dean N. Stahl. Another period of intense collecting occurred during the 1990s, principally led by Charles Bowman, Vernon Phillips, and several New York State mineral clubs that frequently visited the area. In recent years, professional specimen mining has been conducted by Michael Walter and Scott Wallace. Many other collectors have also found excellent specimens during the past fifty or sixty years.

Geology and Origin

The occurrence is a wollastonite skarn that sits between the Grenville marble and a metamorphic rock consisting principally of albite and diopside. Its formation is almost certainly related to the intrusion of the igneous Diana complex about 1.1 billion years ago. It was likely modified by the subsequent regional metamorphism of the Adirondack Lowlands, but the details have not yet been investigated.

Minerals

Most of the minerals listed below occur as sharp crystals embedded in calcite or lining the contact between the albite/diopside metamorphic rock and calcite.

Actinolite, $Ca_2(Mg,Fe^{2+})_5Si_8O_{22}(OH)_2$, occurs rarely as a blue-green coating on diopside crystals. The actinolite is iron-rich and contains significantly more iron than the underlying diopside from which it was probably derived through partial uralitization.

Albite, $NaAlS_3O_8$, occurs as equant to elongated white blocky crystals to 8 cm. The albite shows an antiperthitic texture from internal exsolved lamellae of microcline. Carlsbad and Manebach twins are relatively common locally.

Diopside, $CaMgSi_2O_6$, forms prismatic, forest-green crystals to 20 cm. Many of the crystal faces are pitted or ridged and edges are rounded, but glass-smooth faces also occur.

Fluorapatite, $Ca_5(PO_4)_3F$, occurs as dark blue crystals to 14 cm in calcite, as bright blue crystals with diopside and calcite to 3 cm, and as blue-green crystals with albite and diopside to 8 cm.

Goethite, $FeO(OH)$, usually replaces pyrite, stains the adjacent feldspar, and occasionally forms small clusters of microscopic needles.

Graphite, C, forms tiny tabular crystals to 2 mm, usually in or on albite.

Pyrite, FeS_2, occurs as microscopic euhedral crystals on albite. Most pyrite has weathered to goethite.

Quartz, SiO_2, occurs as white to colorless, rounded crystals to 1 cm that formed from the alteration of wollastonite.

Titanite, $CaTiSiO_5$, occurs as tabular, clove-brown crystals to 12 cm. Although some crystals have a full complement of planar faces, convex faces and stepped growth features are more common. This locality has produced some of the finest titanite crystals from New York State.

Wollastonite, $CaSiO_3$, occurs as well developed, euhedral crystals to 35 cm that are typically wholly or partially altered to a suite of other minerals as described below. The wollastonite crystals are notable for their size and sharpness, ranking among the best in the world.

Zircon, $ZrSiO_4$, occurs as doubly-terminated microscopic brown crystals with graphite and pyrite in the albite.

Pseudomorphs after wollastonite are common, since at least the surface of every wollastonite crystal is somewhat altered.

Diopside and calcite after wollastonite crystals are the most common kind. Many wollastonite crystals have a pale brown rind of varying thickness surrounding a white core of unaltered wollastonite. This rind is composed of a mixture of acicular, pale yellow, iron-rich diopside needles and calcite that appears to have formed from the partial breakdown of wollastonite.

Fig. 67. Albite, titanite. Rose Road Occurrence, Pitcairn, St. Lawrence Co. 4.3 cm. Steven C. Chamberlain collection. SCC

Fig. 69. Diopside, albite. Rose Road Occurrence, Pitcairn, St. Lawrence Co. 4.4 cm. Michael Walter collection. MW

Fig. 68. Diopside, albite, titanite. Rose Road Occurrence, Pitcairn, St. Lawrence Co. 7 cm. Steven C. Chamberlain collection. SCC

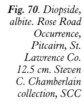

Fig. 70. Diopside, albite. Rose Road Occurrence, Pitcairn, St. Lawrence Co. 12.5 cm. Steven C. Chamberlain collection, SCC

Diopside after wollastonite crystals are pale green with a granular replacement texture resembling a sandstone. Close inspection shows that the diopside is a mosaic of small individual crystal domains.

Quartz after wollastonite crystals are white with a granular replacement texture.

Diopside and quartz after wollastonite crystals show patches of pale green, granular diopside interspersed with patches of white granular quartz.

Similar Occurrences

Farr property just northeast of Natural Bridge (44°04'25"N, 75°28'22"W); Minerva Lake (near 43°47'20"N, 73°58'24"W).

References

BOHLEN, S. R., VALLEY, J. W., and ESSENE, E. J. (1985) Metamorphism in the Adirondacks: I. Petrology, pressure, and temperature. *Journal of Petrology* 26:971-992.

CHAMBERLAIN, S. C. (1985) New occurrences of twinned crystals in St. Lawrence and Lewis Counties, New York. *Rocks & Minerals* 60:285-286.

CHAMBERLAIN S. C., ROBINSON, G. W., and SMITH, C. A. (1987) The occurrence of wollastonite and titanite, Natural Bridge, Lewis County. *Rocks & Minerals* 62:78-89.

CHAMBERLAIN, S. C., KING, V. T., COOKE, D., ROBINSON, G. W., and HOLT, W. (1999) Minerals of the Gouverneur Talc Company No. 4 Quarry (Valentine Deposit), Town of Diana, Lewis County, New York. *Rocks & Minerals* 74:236-249.

CHAMBERLAIN, S. C., WALTER, M. R., ROWE, R., and BAILEY, D. (2009) Investigations of wollastonite from the Rose Road wollastonite deposit, Pitcairn, St. Lawrence County, New York. *Rocks & Minerals* 84:167-168.

GERDES, M. L., and VALLEY, J. W. (1994) Fluid flow and mass transport at the Valentine wollastonite deposit, Adirondack Mountains, New York State. *Journal of Metamorphic Geology* 12:589-608.

LUQUER, L. MCI. (1893) Mineralogical notes: Microcline from Pitcairn, N. Y. *School of Mines Quarterly* 14:328-329.

RIES, H. (1893-1894) On some new forms of wollastonite from New York State. *Transactions of the Academy of Science of New York* 13:146-147.

RIES, H. (1893-1894) Additional note of wollastonite from New York State. *Transactions of the Academy of Science of New York* 13:207-208.

Fig. 71. Fluorapatite, calcite. Rose Road Occurrence, Pitcairn, St. Lawrence Co. 7.4 cm. Steven C. Chamberlain collection. SCC

Fig. 72. Quartz pseudomorph after wollastonite. Rose Road Occurrence, Pitcairn, St. Lawrence Co. 7 cm. Steven C. Chamberlain collection. SCC

RIES, H. (1896) Monoclinic pyroxenes of New York State. *N. Y. Academy of Science Annals* 9:124.

VALLEY, J. W., BOHLEN, S. R., ESSENE, E. J., and LAMB, W. (1990) Metamorphism in the Adirondacks: II. The role of fluids. *Journal of Petrology* 31:555-596.

WALTER, M. R., CHAMBERLAIN, S. C., ROWE, R., and BAILEY, D. (2009) The minerals of the Rose Road wollastonite deposit, Pitcairn, St. Lawrence County, New York. *Rocks & Minerals* 84:454-455.

WALTER, M. (2005) Hardrock digging at Pitcairn. *Rock & Gem* 35(4): 60-63.

WALTER, M. (2007) *Field Collecting Minerals in the Empire State.* Privately published. 212p.

WILLIAMS, G. H. (1885) Cause of the apparently perfect cleavage in American sphene (titanite). *American Journal of Science, Series 3* 29:486-490.

Fig. 73. *Titanite. Rose Road Occurrence, Pitcairn, St. Lawrence Co. 14.5 cm. Steven C. Chamberlain collection. SCC*

Fig. 74. *Wollastonite. Rose Road Occurrence, Pitcairn, St. Lawrence Co. 7 cm. Steven C. Chamberlain collection. SCC*

Bush Farm Brown Tourmaline Locality

Significance

The Bush farm is a world-renown, historic locality for large, well-formed crystals of brown tourmaline (fluor-uvite) and is still producing collector-quality specimens today.

Location and History

The Dale Bush farm (also known as the Stevens, Reese, or Jones farm at various times throughout its history) is located on Welch Road, approximately 2 miles southwest of Richville, in the town of Gouverneur, St. Lawrence County, at 44°23'47"N, 75°25'58"W. Because of the old practice of citing localities by their township names, there exists considerable confusion concerning the locations and histories of brown tourmaline occurrences with localities given simply as "Gouverneur." In addition to the Bush farm, there are several old marble quarries just south of the village of Gouverneur that produced well-formed crystals of brown tourmaline, as well as several other lesser-known localities near the village of Richville, but in the town of De Kalb. In his 1842 treatise on the mineralogy of New York, Beck describes a locality for "… brown tourmaline, in perfect crystals, associated with tremolite …" that fits the Bush farm perfectly, but gives the locality as "… at Richville, in the town of De Kalb…" (Beck 1842,

359) Thus, whether Beck's description cites the wrong township or a different locality remains unclear.

It may be that credit for the discovery of this famous locality is owed to Floyd Hamlin, a resident of Richville, circa 1860 or before. In a little-known publication *Crystals and Gold* by Roselle Cross, a Congregational Church Pastor, mineral collector, and boyhood resident of Richville, it states:

> A new family moved into the house across the road from my father's. I heard that the man was a collector of minerals … That mineral neighbor, Floyd Hamlin, and myself became life long friends … He told me of a place in Gouverneur, three miles away, where I could find tremolite and brown tourmaline … Mr. Nims of Philadelphia, New York … asked me to show him the place … I did so and received a shilling for it and for helping him lug a lot of specimens out to the road. He afterwards extensively worked the locality and probably sold several thousand dollars worth of single crystals and clusters of beautiful translucent brown tourmalines from that place. Some splendid ones went to Hamilton College. It became a famous locality. I learn that this year (1902) it has again been extensively and successfully worked. (Cross 1903, 38–39)

Since then, many hundreds of mineral collectors have visited this famous locality, where excellent specimens are still being found today.

Fig. 75. Diopside, talc. Bush Farm, Richville, St. Lawrence Co. 10 cm. Root collection, New York State Museum. SCC

Fig. 76. Fluor-uvite. Bush Farm, Richville, St. Lawrence Co. 4.3 cm. Steven C. Chamberlain collection. MW

Fig. 77. Fluor-uvite. Bush Farm, Richville, St. Lawrence Co. 8 cm. New York State Museum collection. SN

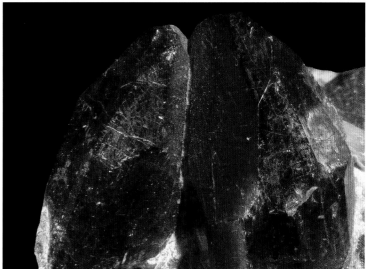

Fig. 79. Fluor-uvite, Bush Farm, Richville, St. Lawrence Co. 1.5 cm. New York State Museum collection. ML

Fig. 78. Fluor-uvite. Bush Farm, Richville, St. Lawrence Co. 5.8 cm. New York State Museum. MW

Fig. 80. Tremolite, calcite. Bush Farm, Richville, St. Lawrence Co. 7.3 cm. Steven C. Chamberlain collection. MW

Geology and Origin

Overall, the geology of the Bush farm tourmaline locality is similar to that of the West Pierrepont tremolite occurrence or De Kalb gem diopside locality (q.v.). The tourmaline, in association with diopside, tremolite, and calcite, occurs in pockets in a band of metasedimentary calc-silicate rock in contact with Grenville Marble. The boron required for the tourmaline was probably present in the original sediments, as there is no apparent granitic source nearby.

Minerals

Twelve minerals have been reported from this locality, but only four have been found in collector-quality specimens: diopside, fluorapatite, fluor-uvite, and tremolite.

Diopside, $CaMgSi_2O_6$, occurs as opaque, white, elongated pinacoidal crystals to several centimeters associated with tremolite and fluor-uvite. Often the surfaces of the crystals appear soft and weathered, though some that occur embedded in calcite are fresher and may make collectible specimens.

Fluorapatite, $Ca_5(PO_4)_3F$, has been found in grayish blue, terminated hexagonal prisms up to 6 cm, most often associated with diopside or tremolite. It is not common.

Fluor-uvite, $CaMg_3(MgAl_5)(BO_3)_3[Si_6O_{18}][F_3(OH)]$, occurs as complex, doubly-terminated, cinnamon-brown prismatic crystals from 2 to 15 cm in length in open pockets in the calc-silicate rock or embedded in white calcite with tremolite. The crystals are complexly terminated, equant to elongated on [001], and show dramatic hemimorphic development. Although of good color, most are too fractured to afford gemstones. Hundreds of fine specimens have been found over the years, though the best and largest is probably that collected by C. D. Nims, originally in the Oren Root collection at Hamilton College and now in the New York State Museum. Using new analyses and the new tourmaline nomenclature recently published, Dr. Marian Lupulescu has determined that most of this tourmaline is fluor-uvite.

Tremolite, $Ca_2Mg_5Si_8O_{22}(OH)_2$, is perhaps the most common species found at the Bush farm, and after fluor-uvite, the one of greatest interest to collectors. Terminated, glassy white crystals over 10 cm across have been found embedded in calcite or in aggregates with fluor-uvite and/or diopside. Cleavage sections of even larger crystals have been found, though most are smaller.

Similar Occurrences

West Pierrepont tremolite occurrence (44°29'26"N, 75°02'19"W); Seven Springs area (44°34'51"N, 74°51'35"W); De Kalb achroite (colorless tourmaline) locality (near 44°28'27"N, 75°19'43"W); Hurlbut farm (44°29'04"N, 75°26'48"W); Hall farm (44°26'03"N, 75°29'03"W).

References

AGAR, W. M. (1921) The minerals of St. Lawrence, Jefferson and Lewis Counties, New York. *American Mineralogist* 6(10):148-53, 6(11):158-64.

BECK, L. C. (1842) *Mineralogy of New-York*. Thurlow Weed, Printer to the State, Albany, New York: 359.

CROSS, R. T. (1903) *Crystals and Gold*. The Nebraska Newspaper Union, York, Nebraska. 196p.

CUSHING, H. P. and NEWLAND, D. H. (1925) Geology of the Gouverneur Quadrangle. *New York State Museum Bulletin No. 259*:20.

DUNN, P. (1977) Uvite, a new (old) member of the tourmaline group and its implications for collectors. *Mineralogical Record* 8:100-08.

HENRY, D. J., NOVAK, M., HAWTHORNE, F. C., ERTL, A., DUTROW, B. L., UHER, P., and PEZZOTTA, F. (2011) Nomenclature of the tourmaline-supergroup minerals. *American Mineralogist* 96:895-913.

STAHL, D. N. (1985) The morphology of tourmaline (uvite) crystals from three localities in northern New York (abstract). *Rocks & Minerals* 60:288.

West Pierrepont Tremolite Occurrence

Significance

This is probably the best representative locality of the widespread tremolite mineralization in St. Lawrence County, NY. Besides producing excellent green tremolite specimens, it has also been the source of some of the finest tourmalines found anywhere in New York State. The locality is extensive with much unexplored and unexploited mineralized area and is an ongoing source of excellent specimens and mineralogical surprises.

Location and History

The extended locality occupies an east-west ridge east of the three corners at West Pierrepont and south of Selleck Road about one mile from its western end. The GPS coordinates of the clearing used for parking are 44°29'26"N, 75°02'19"W. This clearing is about the middle of the east-west extent of the mineralized area.

In the early 1960s, a local collector, the late Robert Dow, was prompted to investigate the site based on information from his father-in-law who was doing exploration for the Hanna Ore Company that was investigating the Clifton Mine deposit. Dow shared the information with fellow collectors Schuyler Alverson and George W. Robinson who further disseminated the information. In 1969, George W. Robinson and Ray Buyce from the New York State Museum, armed with a letter signed by Governor Nelson Rockefeller giving them permission to drill and blast in a state forest, collected the first important tremolite specimens. By the late 1960s, mineral clubs were taking field trips to the site and Robinson and Alverson included the locality in their 1971 guidebook.

The gemmy, dark brown fluor-uvite crystals from this locality are a favorite with collectors. Starting in 1969, first Ivan McIntosh and then Ronald Waddell collected numerous excellent tourmaline specimens west of the clearing. In 1974, Steven C. Chamberlain found another occurrence for high-quality tourmaline crystals nearby. In 1991, Terry Holmes discovered a third occurrence of tourmaline a bit farther west and collected some of the finest fluor-uvite crystals yet produced. In 1994, Charlie and Larry Bowman found the largest tourmalines from the locality to date on top of the ridge to the east of the clearing. In 2006, Michael Walter and Scott Wallace found a fourth significant occurrence of tourmaline just west of where Terry Holmes had dug in 1991.

Fig. 82. Fluor-uvite. West Pierrepont, St. Lawrence Co. 2.1 cm. New York State Museum. ML

Fig. 83. Microcline pseudomorph after marialite. West Pierrepont, St. Lawrence Co. 20 cm. Steven C. Chamberlain collection. SCC

Fig. 81. Fluor-uvite. West Pierrepont, St. Lawrence Co. 6 cm. Steven C. Chamberlain collection. MW

Some other significant specimens besides the green tremolite and brown fluor-uvite were also discovered. In 1984, Steven C. Chamberlain and William Condon found a pod of colorless tremolite at the eastern tip of the mineralized ridge. In 1985, Ivan McIntosh collected a number of albite pseudomorphs after marialite from an excavation on top of the ridge to the east of the clearing. In 1999, Michael Walter discovered a single pocket of sulfide mineralization similar to the fracture-filling mineralization in the Balmat District adjacent to the tourmaline occurrences west of the clearing. In 2010, Donald Carlin, Jr. and Michael Walter excavated an unusual occurrence of phlogopite triplets at a site on the western edge of the ridge to the east of the clearing. These unusual mica twins were accompanied by heulandite, marialite, albite, microcline, and tremolite.

This extensive locality remains only partially explored. It is very likely that future collecting will continue to yield more, better, and different mineral specimens.

Geology and Origin

This locality is only one of a number of tremolite occurrences in the vicinity that were formed by the metamorphism of silica-rich dolomitic limestones and evaporites during the late Precambrian. The detailed variability of mineral associations at the various pits and trenches across the locality probably reflects local differences in the compositions of the precursor sediments. The westernmost edge of the mineralized region abuts a large dome of Precambrian Hyde School granite-gneiss that intruded near the beginning of the regional metamorphism, whereas most of the minerals present formed toward the end of the regional metamorphism, especially the tremolite and fluor-uvite. Thus, the mineralization was probably little affected by the granite intrusion.

Significant exposures of the Precambrian Grenville marble are evident as white fine-grained calcite that is in sharp contrast to the coarser-grained, pink to tan to orange calcite formed by the metamorphic reactions that produced the various silicates with which it is in contact.

Tremolite, fluor-uvite, diopside, pyrite, phlogopite, quartz, microcline, albite, and marialite are probably prograde minerals that were formed during the height of regional metamorphism, whereas talc and the minerals that have replaced marialite are probably retrograde minerals that formed toward the end of the period of regional metamorphism. Allanite-(Ce), an unidentified REE-silicate mineral that is probably percleveite-(Ce), and chalcopyrite appear to represent later hydrothermal mineralization through fractures. Goethite formed from the weathering of pyrite; and heulandite, from the breakdown of marialite.

Minerals

The following minerals have been identified from sites across this locality. There is much variation locally, although tremolite is almost always present.

Albite, $NaAlSi_3O_8$, occurs as white equant crystals to 1 cm and as creamy white pseudomorphs after marialite. The replacement texture is a mosaic of equant domains with some open interstitial spaces that sometimes contain rare-earth minerals.

Allanite-(Ce), $CaCeFeAl_2(Si_2O_7)(SiO_4)O(OH)$, occurs as microscopic skeletal and prismatic crystals.

Calcite, $CaCO_3$, occurs as buff-colored, fine-grained marble; as coarse, pink to orange masses in contact with tremolite and other crystallized silicates; and as small white rhombohedral crystals associated with chalcopyrite.

Chalcopyrite, $CuFeS_2$, occurs as elongated bisphenoidal crystals with calcite and pyrite in the mineralized cavities in the marble. Some crystals have more complex morphology. All are covered by a thin brown coating that appears to be goethite. Some chalcopyrite crystals have tiny sprays or rosettes of bright green malachite crystals on them.

Diopside, $CaMgSi_2O_6$, occurs as a pale green, fine-grained rock and as prismatic crystals of the same color to 13 centimeters or more in length. Most diopside crystals at this locality show prominent basal parting. Many have a dull surface, are overgrown with tremolite, sometimes epitactically, or partially replaced by tremolite or talc.

Fluorapatite, $Ca_5(PO_4)_3F$, is known from only a handful of specimens. Crystals are medium green and consist of a hexagonal prism, basal pinacoid and hexagonal bipyramid. The largest crystal we have observed is about 1 centimeter.

Fluor-uvite, $CaMg_3(MgAl_5)(BO_3)_3[Si_6O_{18}][F_3(OH)]$, occurs as dark yellow-brown to reddish-brown lustrous crystals to 16 centimeters that may appear nearly black in hand specimens. The crystallography is complex and often difficult to decipher because many of the crystals show growth distortions, and the hemimorphic nature of tourmaline means that singly terminated crystals could be top-side up or bottom-side up. The crystal forms present include: $a\{100\}$, $b\{010\}$, $m\{110\}$, $r\{101\}$, $o\{021\}$, $e\{012\}$, $u\{321\}$, $t\{211\}$, $s\{210\}$, $z\{011\}$ and $z'\{01\bar{1}\}$. Doubly terminated crystals often show prominent hemimorphism. Using new analyses and the newly published tourmaline nomenclature, Dr. Marian Lupulescu has determined that the tourmaline species is fluor-uvite.

Goethite, $FeO(OH)$, occurs across the locality as stains from the oxidation of pyrite and as goethite pseudomorphs after pyrite. Goethite also forms thin coatings on microscopic chalcopyrite crystals.

Heulandite-Ca, $(Ca_{0.5},Na,K)_9[Al_9Si_{27}]_{72}\cdot24H_2O$, occurs as aggregates of translucent gray crystals to several mm on altered marialite.

Malachite, $Cu_2(CO_3)(OH)_2$, occurs as bright green rosettes and sprays of acicular crystals perched on chalcopyrite crystals.

Marialite, $Na_4Al_3Si_9O_{24}Cl$, occurs as prismatic crystals to 10 centimeters in complex clusters to 15 or 20 centimeters. When unaltered, the marialite is medium lavender. Most crystals, however, are completely altered to creamy white albite as in the eastern parts of the locality or to white to tan microcline, at least on their surfaces, in the western parts of the locality.

Microcline, $KAlSi_3O_8$, occurs as white equant to prismatic crystals to 6 cm. It also commonly replaces marialite toward the western end of the locality where it may contain minor barium and be interspersed with oriented layers of magnesium-rich muscovite.

Phlogopite, $KMg_3AlSi_3O_{10}(OH)_2$, from this locality contains significant fluorine and some might actually be fluorophlogopite. It occurs as prismatic brown crystals to 4 cm and occasionally as tabular plates to 10 cm. It is also found as triplets to several centimeters associated with altered scapolite, microcline, tremolite, and heulandite-

Ca. These unusual twins seem to result from elongation along the *a*-axis and twinning by rotation around both the [310] and [-310] axes, with suppression of three of the resulting six blades to form a triplet. The triplets are all oriented overgrowths on untwinned pseudohexagonal phlogopite crystals.

Pyrite, FeS_2, occurs as anhedral to euhedral masses, largely in the pale green, fine-grained diopside rock. Euhedral crystals are typically distorted, making it difficult to identify which forms are present. Most pyrite is altered, at least on the surface, to brown goethite. In the mineralized cavities in the marble, pyrite occurs with chalcopyrite as microscopic brassy cubic crystals on calcite crystals.

Quartz, SiO_2, is a relatively common mineral at the locality, but rarely in particularly good crystals. Most are translucent gray to a smoky-brown color. When quartz occurs as euhedral crystals, the prism faces frequently are slightly bowed inward between the prism edges, and the rhombohedral terminal faces are frequently rounded. Most quartz crystals are less than 3 centimeters in length.

Talc, $Mg_3Si_4O_{10}(OH)_2$, occurs as a white to tan alteration of diopside forming talc pseudomorphs after diopside.

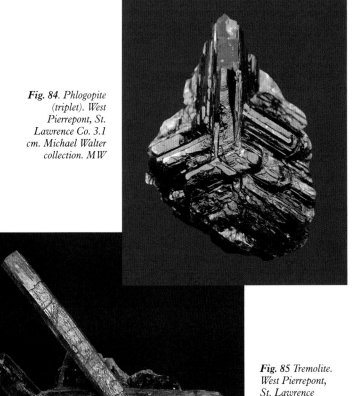

Fig. 84. Phlogopite (triplet). West Pierrepont, St. Lawrence Co. 3.1 cm. Michael Walter collection. MW

Fig. 85 Tremolite. West Pierrepont, St. Lawrence Co. 8 cm. Steven C. Chamberlain collection. MW

Fig. 86. Tremolite. West Pierrepont, St. Lawrence Co. 5.6 cm. Steven C. Chamberlain collection. MW

Tremolite, $Ca_2Mg_5Si_8O_{22}OH)_2$, occurs as colorless to gray-green, medium to dark green, to almost black crystals to 10 centimeters or more in length, although most crystals are less than 3 centimeters. The lateral pinacoids, $a\{100\}$ and $b\{010\}$, and four monoclinic prisms: $m\{110\}$, $r\{011\}$, $d\{210\}$, and $e\{120\}$ are the most common crystal forms. Typical crystals have glassy, variably striated $\{hk0\}$ prism faces terminated with dull r faces. Tremolite crystals range from tabular crystals flattened along the c-axis with dominating r faces to columnar crystals elongated along the c-axis to tabular crystals flattened along the a-axis. Single crystals and clusters of several crystals with no visible points of attachment are relatively common, apparently having formed in, and subsequently weathered out of, calcite.

Unidentified Rare-Earth Silicate occurs as blocky, equant crystals in interstitial spaces between domains of albite in albite pseudomorphs after marialite.

Similar Occurrences

Hall farm (44°26'03"N, 75°29'03"W); Moore farm (44°28'04"N, 75°07'02"W); Hurlbut farm (44°29'04"N, 75°26'48"W); Chiarenzelli prospect (44°34'58"N, 74°51'23"W); Seven Springs area (44°34'51"N, 74°51'35"W); Bush farm (44°23'47"N, 75°25'58"W); De Kalb achroite (colorless tourmaline) locality on the Murtey farm (near 44°28'27"N, 75°19'43"W); O'Brien farm (44°28'28"N, 75°07'29"W); De Kalb gem diopside locality (Mitchell farm) (44°27'01"N, 75°19'36"W).

References

CHAMBERLAIN, S. C., ROBINSON, G. W., WALTER, M., and BAILEY, D. G. Selleck Road exposures of tremolite and uvite, West Pierrepont, St. Lawrence County, New York. *Rocks & Minerals* (in press as of this writing).

HENRY, D. J., NOVAK, M., HAWTHORNE, F. C., ERTL, A., DUTROW, B. L., UHER, P. and PEZZOTTA, F. (2011) Nomenclature of the tourmaline-supergroup minerals. *American Mineralogist* 96:895-913.

ROBINSON, G. W., and ALVERSON, S. (1971) Minerals of the St. Lawrence Valley. Privately published. 42p.

STAHL, D. N. (1985) The morphology of tourmaline (uvite) crystals from three localities in northern New York. *Rocks & Minerals* 60:288.

De Kalb Gem Diopside Locality

Significance

Few places in the world have produced crystals of diopside that equal those from this classic North American locality. Lustrous, transparent, green, gem-quality crystals 5–10 cm long, as well as faceted gemstones of 10–15 carats can be seen in many of the world's major mineral museums. Their overall high quality and deep green color place the De Kalb crystals alongside those from Burma, Tanzania, and China as viable contenders for "world's finest."

Location and History

The De Kalb gem diopside locality is located on a northeasterly-trending ridge approximately 3.5 miles northeast of the village of Richville in De Kalb Township, St. Lawrence County, NY at (44°27'01"N, 75°19'36"W). It is unclear exactly when or by whom the first diopside crystals were collected, but it was probably in the early 1880s by Calvin Mitchell, a farmer who owned the land at that time. In 1892, George F. Kunz wrote in *Gems and Precious Stones of North America*:

> Some very large crystals were found in 1884, several of which were over 3 inches long and 1 inch thick, with clear spots of gem material giving promise of cut gems weighing 20 to 30 carats each. (Kunz 1892, 151)

Such fine crystals were unprecedented at the time and soon caught the attention of collectors, gemologists, and scientists alike. Vom Rath described crystals from the locality as early as 1886, as did Ries in 1896. Both Dana and Hintze referenced diopside from De Kalb in their texts, *System of Mineralogy* and *Handbuch der Mineralogie*.

In 1899, the famous New York City mineral dealer George L. English secured the right to mine diopside, but apparently little work was done and the locality eventually became "lost" until it was rediscovered by Terry Szenics in 1967. With the aid of a gasoline-powered drill and hand tools, Szenics was able to open at least one worthwhile pocket, and fine crystals were once again available in the marketplace after a half-century absence. In 1971, the property was purchased by Schuyler Alverson, George Robinson, and Robert Dow, who worked it sporadically over the next two decades. While numerous small pockets were discovered during that time, one found on June 6, 1971, was particularly noteworthy. Alverson and Robinson (together with his wife Susan) had spent most of the day cleaning off a promising area in preparation for drilling, when just before dark, a small pocket was uncovered. The sun was setting and the three were tired, but since the day's labor had produced virtually no specimens, it was decided to spend "just five minutes" investigating the pocket. Four hours later and still working with the aid of a Coleman lantern and truck headlights, the happy trio had recovered over two hundred gem-quality crystals, ranging in size from 1 to 7 cm—clearly the best find since George English had worked the locality seventy years ago.

In 2004, the property was sold to its current owner, David Kords, who continues to work it for specimens and gem rough. To date, only a relatively small volume of the total mineralized rock available has been excavated, and the outlook for future specimen production is good, but will likely require a small scale mining operation to be effective.

Geology and Origin

This locality is one of several geologically similar occurrences in the area that were formed by the regional metamorphism of siliceous dolomitic limestone in late Precambrian (Grenvillian) time. Temperatures and pressures probably peaked in the upper amphibolite to lower granulite facies. The host rock at the occurrence consists of a 1–2 meter thick layer of pure white massive diopside sandwiched between two layers of a calc-silicate schist composed predominantly of quartz and tremolite with widely scattered, rusty, subhedral crystals of pyrite. Locally, quartz may exceed tremolite, with the rock grading into a quartzite. This whole sequence dips approximately 45° to the northwest and is transected by joints and tremolite veinlets perpendicular to its strike. It is along these veinlets and within the massive white diopside unit that most of the gem pockets tend to occur. It should be noted, however, that not all pockets contain diopside crystals. Most are filled with tremolite needles, minor calcite and a soft clay-like mixture of talc and quartz, or pseudomorphs of tremolite after diopside. These later minerals probably formed during a period of retrograde metamorphism, as temperatures waned, producing conditions under which the earlier-formed diopside was no longer stable and was replaced by tremolite, and the tremolite eventually by talc + quartz + calcite.

Fig. 87. Diopside. Mitchell Farm, De Kalb, St. Lawrence Co. 3.4 cm. Canadian Museum of Nature. GWR

Fig. 89. Diopside. Mitchell Farm, De Kalb, St. Lawrence Co. 5.1 cm. New York State Museum. GBG

Fig. 88. Diopside, quartz. Mitchell Farm, De Kalb, St. Lawrence Co. 5 cm. Canadian Museum of Nature. SN

Fig. 90. Tremolite. Mitchell Farm, De Kalb, St. Lawrence Co. 9 cm. New York State Museum. ML

Minerals

Only seven species have been identified from this locality: albite, calcite, diopside, pyrite, quartz, talc, and tremolite. Datolite has been reported but cannot be confirmed. Of these, only albite, diopside, quartz, and tremolite are of collector interest; the other species occurring in either massive form or subhedral to anhedral crystals.

Albite, $NaAlSi_3O_8$, is rare at this locality and occurs as tabular, etched, cream-white crystals to 2.5 cm.

Diopside, $CaMgSi_2O_6$, is the mineral of primary interest at this locality and occurs as lustrous, transparent, prismatic crystals up to 10 cm, though most are less than half that size. Smaller crystals tend to be pale green, while larger ones are a darker, richer green, making them desirable as gem rough. Most crystals are found already detached from their pocket walls, making good matrix specimens difficult to come by. The crystals typically have smooth, lustrous prism and pinacoid faces parallel to [001] zone, but somewhat etched or pitted terminations that are typically selectively coated with talc. Common forms include $\{1\bar{0}0\}$, $\{010\}$, $\{0\bar{0}1\}$, $\{\bar{1}10\}$ and $\{111\}$; less common are $\{101\}$, $\{011\}$, $\{\bar{1}11\}$, $\{\bar{2}21\}$, $\{221\}$ and $\{\bar{3}11\}$.

Quartz, SiO_2, is frequently found as etched, gray to milky blebs or subhedral crystals in some of the pockets, or occasionally as transparent, colorless, prismatic crystals to 2 cm with or without cauliflower-like inclusions of talc, associated with and growing on diopside crystals. Good quartz specimens are uncommon.

Tremolite, $Ca_2Mg_5Si_8O_{22}(OH)_2$, occurs as colorless to gray, prismatic crystals up to 10 cm, but are seldom terminated, since they tend to bridge the pocket walls. Perhaps of greater interest to the collector are the tremolite pseudomorphs after diopside that occur all too frequently in the larger pockets from which one had hoped to have found unaltered diopside crystals instead. Often the tremolite appears epitactically oriented on the diopside, with the *b* and *c* axes in the tremolite parallel to the same axes in the diopside.

Similar Occurrences

Hall farm (44°26'03"N, 75°29'03"W); Moore farm (44°28'04"N, 75°07'02"W); Hurlbut farm (44°29'04"N, 75°26'48"W), O'Brien farm (44°28'28"N, 75°07'29"W); West Pierrepont tremolite occurrence (44°29'26"N, 75°02'19"W). Small glassy crystals of diopside have been found at all these localities, but none in larger, dark green, gem-quality crystals like those from De Kalb.

References
CHAMBERLAIN, S. C., ROBINSON, G. W., WALTER, M., and BAILEY, D. G. Selleck Road exposures of tremolite and uvite, West Pierrepont, St. Lawrence County, New York. *Rocks & Minerals* (in press at the time of this writing).

DANA, E. S. (1892) *The System of Mineralogy*. Sixth edition, John Wiley and Sons, New York.

HINTZE, C. (1896) *Handbuch der Mineralogie*. Zweiter Band, Silicate und Titanate. Verlag von Veit und Comp., Leipzig.

KUNZ, G. F. (1892). *Gems and Precious Stones of North America*. Second edition, reprinted (1968) by Dover Publications Inc., New York.

RIES, H. (1896) The Monoclinic Pyroxenes of New York State. *Annals of the New York Academy of Science* 9:124-80, and Plates XIII-XVI.

ROBINSON, G. W. (1973). De Kalb Diopside. *Lapidary Journal* 27:1040-42, 1058-59.

ROBINSON, G. W. (1990). Famous Mineral Localities: De Kalb, New York. *Mineralogical Record* 21:535-41.

SZENICS, T. (1968). World-famous lost American diopside locality rediscovered. *Lapidary Journal* 21:1232-39.

VOM RATH, G. (1886). Diopside from De Kalb, N. Y. *Sitzber. Niederrh. Ges. Für Nat. u. Heilk.* 224.

VOM RATH, G. (1888). Über Diopsid von De Kalb, N. Y. *Zeitschrift für Krystallographie und Mineralogie* 13:598.

Russell Danburite Occurrence

Significance

This was the first North American locality to produce danburite crystals and provided important early descriptive information on the species. It was also the first of several high-temperature borosilicate mineral occurrences formed during granulite facies metamorphism around the periphery of the Adirondack Highlands to be discovered, and is one of a growing number of Precambrian-hosted localities in New York to contain late-stage, rare-earth minerals formed by hydrothermal solutions.

Location and History

The danburite occurrence near Russell is located on the former Van Buskirk farm at 44°22'10"N, 75°11'14"W, approximately 4.5 miles south of the Village of Russell in the Town of Russell in St. Lawrence County. The locality was brought to light when noted local mineral dealer Chester D. Nims sent specimens to Yale University for identification. Professors George J. Brush and Edward S. Dana determined that the mineral was danburite, then a new species just recently described from Danbury, CT. The Russell occurrence provided excellent crystals and permitted them to publish the first detailed paper on the crystallography of danburite in 1880. Many specimens were produced in the nineteenth century and found their way into collections world wide. During the twentieth century, only sporadic collecting was permitted and the occurrence was nearly lost. In 2009, limited collecting sanctioned by new property owners exposed a second and third pod of danburite mineralization.

Geology and Origin

The occurrence sits just east of the border between two local geological provinces—the Adirondack Lowlands to the west and the Adirondack Highlands to the east. In the lowlands, which experienced regional amphibolite-facies metamorphism, various tourmaline species are the most common boron-containing minerals. In the highlands, which achieved higher grade, granulite-facies metamorphism (650–700°C and 6–7 kilobars), anhydrous boron-containing minerals

formed where that element was available. The Russell danburite occurrence is one of these. Presumably boron was provided by Precambrian evaporite layers in the extensive sequence of metasediments in the Adirondack Lowlands or from the nearby Dana Hill gabbro.

Danburite crystals occur in pods hosted in a layered danburite-diopside metasediment. Crystallized minerals occur in the host rock along the walls of each pod and are also found suspended in their calcite cores, which have mostly weathered away. Minerals of interest to collectors appear to have crystallized in three stages. Prograde minerals formed at the height of regional metamorphism and were followed by retrograde minerals that formed as the temperature and pressure decreased. Tectonic activity following the retrograde metamorphism fractured the brittle silicates, providing space for hydrothermal mineralization that occurred much later after the calcite cores had largely dissolved away.

Fig. 91. Danburite. Russell, St. Lawrence Co. 5.5 cm.
Steven C. Chamberlain collection. SCC

Fig. 92. Danburite. Russell, St. Lawrence Co. 7 cm.
Steven C. Chamberlain collection. SCC

Minerals

The suite of primary, or prograde metamorphic minerals includes calcite, danburite, diopside, fluorapatite, microcline, phlogopite, titanite, quartz, and scapolite. The suite of retrograde metamorphic minerals includes datolite, dravite, quartz replacing danburite, and tremolite. Late-stage hydrothermal minerals include quartz (variety amethyst), dravite, pyrite, an unidentified Y-rich silicate and an unidentified Ce-rich silicate. Only crystallized species of interest to mineral collectors are described in more detail.

Datolite, $CaBSiO_4(OH)$, occurs as microscopic white crystals in fractures and as patches on danburite crystals.

Danburite, $CaB_2(SiO_4)_2$, occurs as colorless to tan to yellow crystals to 10 cm. Crystals with square cross-sections are dominated by two sets of lateral pinacoids, while those with diamond-shaped cross-sections are dominated by orthorhombic prisms. Many c-pinacoid terminations are modified by orthorhombic dipyramids. Crystals collected before 2009 from the original pod tend to be colorless to tan, internally fractured, with low surface luster. Crystals collected from the second and third pods are generally only a few centimeters long, but have fewer fractures and are often transparent with a honey-yellow color. Moreover, they tend to form complex aggregates of crystals, which are largely unknown from the first pod.

Diopside, $CaMgSi_2O_6$, occurs as transparent emerald green crystals and opaque gray-green crystals to several centimeters.

Dravite, $NaMg_3Al_6(BO_3)_3[Si_6O_{18}](OH)_4$, occurs as dark brown striated crystals terminated by a trigonal pyramid and as late-stage crusts of parallel-growth crystals on danburite. The dravite in the matrix and lining the walls of the pods formed as a retrograde alteration of danburite.

Fluorapatite, $Ca_5(PO4)_3F$, occurs as prismatic green to blue-gray crystals to 3 cm.

Pyrite, FeS_2, occurs as late-stage pyritohedral crystals to 5 mm on danburite.

Phlogopite, $KMg_3AlSi_3O_{10}(OH)_2$, forms dark brown, iron-rich (5 wt % FeO) tabular crystals to several centimeters.

Quartz, SiO_2, in the prograde suite forms rounded translucent prisms of milky to smoky color. Retrograde quartz rarely replaces danburite. Late-stage quartz is sharply crystallized, including transparent purple amethyst crystals to 4 mm.

Titanite, $CaTiOSiO_4$, occurs as transparent clove-brown crystals to several millimeters and dark brown, almost black, tabular crystals to a centimeter or more.

Tremolite, $Ca_2Mg_5Si_8O_{22}(OH)_2$, occurs as pale green overgrowths on diopside and as scattered small crystals, sometimes spanning open fractures in danburite.

Unidentified Rare-Earth Mineral 1 is a yttrium, calcium, alumino-silicate with lesser amounts of cerium and neodymium. It forms microscopic flattened platy crystals on tremolite.

Unidentified Rare-Earth Mineral 2 (possibly allanite-(Ce)) is a cerium, iron, calcium, alumino-silicate with lesser amounts of lanthanum. It forms microscopic blocky prismatic crystals on tremolite.

Similar Occurrences

Serendibite in a drill core along the northern border of the Town of Russell (44°30'08"N, 75°08'55"W); vonsenite from the Jayville Iron mines (44°09'38"N, 75°11'20"W); prismatine from Moose River (43°36'37"N, 75°10'01"W); serendibite and sinhalite from near Johnsburg (43°33'45"N, 74°00'49"W); kornerupine from Warrensburg (43°32'37"N, 73°49'35"W); and stillwellite-(Ce) from Mineville (44°05'23"N, 73°31'31"W). All these uncommon, high-temperature, boron-containing minerals formed around the periphery of the Adirondack Highlands under presumably similar geological conditions.

References

BRUSH, G. J. and DANA, E. S. (1880) On crystallized danburite from Russell, St. Lawrence County, New York. *American Journal of Science* 120:111-118.

CHAMBERLAIN, S. C., LUPULESCU, M., BAILEY, D. G., and CARLIN, D. M., Jr. (2011) Classic danburite locality near Russell, St. Lawrence County, New York: New collecting and new research. *Rocks & Minerals* 86:175-176.

CHAMBERLAIN, S. C., LUPULESCU, M., and BAILEY, D. G. The Classic Danburite Occurrence near Russell, St. Lawrence County, New York. *Rocks & Minerals* (in preparation at the time of this writing).

EDWARDS, R. L. and ESSENE, E. J. (1988) Pressure, temperature and C-O-H fluid fugacities across the amphibolite-granulite transition, northwest Adirondack Mountains, New York. *Journal of Petrology* 29:39-72.

DARLING, R. S., FLORENCE, F. P., LESTER, G. W., and WHITNEY, P. R. (2004) Petrogenesis of prismatine-bearing metapelitic gneisses along the Moose River, west-central Adirondacks, NY. In: Proterozoic tectonic evolution of the Grenville orogen in North America. (Ed. R. P. Tollo) *GSA Memoir* 197:325-336.

GREW, E. S. (1996) Borosilicates (exclusive of tourmaline) and boron in rock-forming minerals in metamorphic environments. In "Boron: mineralogy, petrology and geochemistry" (Eds. Grew E. S. and Annovitz, L. M.), *Reviews in Mineralogy* 33:387-503.

Pierrepont Black Tourmaline Occurrence

Significance

The distinctive lustrous black tourmaline crystals from this locality are common in mineral collections all over the world. Except for the various occurrences of the Herkimer diamond variety of quartz, no other locality in New York State has produced as many fine mineral specimens over so long a period of time.

Location and History

The Pierrepont black tourmaline locality is on the current Bower Powers farm about 1.25 miles north of the four-corners of Pierrepont, in St. Lawrence County, just north of Post Road where it ends at Leonard Brook. Contemporary collectors group the various mineralized sites at this locality into three areas: the four stream-side veins at 44°33'28"N, 75°01'14"W; the various pits and trenches on the top of the hill at 44°33'32"N, 75°01'12"W; and the southeastern area at 44°33'24"N, 75°01'03"W.

The occurrence on the top of the hill seems to have been discovered first. The earliest published mention of the locality appears to be in a book by R. T. Cross. In it, he relates how he and his father were led to the locality in the early 1850s:

> BLACK TOURMALINE. My father took me with him once to a religious meeting twenty-five miles from home, up on the hills of Pierrepont. At the farmer's house where we stopped I saw a shining black crystal of tourmaline. In reply to my inquiry as to where it came from they said it was found in abundance near an old saw mill about half a mile distant. The next morning they took us to the place. I dug the black brilliants for a half hour or so and then a thunder storm drove us away ... I gave some to a farmer in a distant part of the county. Mr. Nims saw them and followed up the clue until he found the locality, and from that place also he sold wagon loads of tourmaline crystals. It has been a famous locality, for no blacker, or more brilliant, or more sharply cut crystals of tourmaline are found in this world. I visited the place in 1871, 1875, 1883, and 1890, and always came with hundreds of specimens, good, bad, and indifferent. (Cross 1903, 40)

The locality, however, had not yet come to the notice of Franklin Hough when he published his extensive listing of minerals found in St. Lawrence and Franklin Counties in 1853.

In 1921, William Agar published a first-hand account of the top of the hill area:

> PIERREPONT BLACK TOURMALINE LOCALITY. This is another famous collecting ground. It is doubtless the locality from which most of the black tourmaline in the mineral collections of the country has come ... The tourmaline occurs as a band running from the brook intermittently up the hill for about 150 meters. A great many pits have been blasted in it, but it still forms a very conspicuous black band on the slope. Clusters of brilliant black crystals are abundant and doubly terminated, stubby, polar crystals can with care be dug out. They occur with quartz, some calcite, phlogopite, and pyroxene in good square crystals. These grow more abundant as the band is followed up the hill. (Agar 1921, 161)

In the 1970s, an open vein of smoky quartz and calcite crystals was discovered in the middle of the top of the hill and worked extensively into the 1980s and then again starting in 2006.

Fig. 93. Dravite, Waddell Trench, Powers Farm, Pierrepont, St. Lawrence Co. 6.8 cm. Steven C. Chamberlain collection. MW

The southeastern area consists of a hill falling off to the east into a wetland. This area is colloquially referred to as the swamp and was a popular collecting area in the middle of the twentieth century, but has since then largely been ignored. It has probably not been very thoroughly explored.

There are four stream-side veins. From north to south, they are known colloquially as the Wallace-Carlin vein, the Waddell vein, the middle vein, and the phosphate vein. The Waddell vein was discovered in the late 1950s by Ronald Waddell, worked, and then abandoned for forty years. Starting in 2005, it was professionally worked by Michael Walter and Scott Wallace who extended it almost to the stream. Subsequently, Walter worked the phosphate vein and the Middle vein, and Wallace and Donald Carlin, Jr., worked the Wallace-Carlin vein. There are probably more roughly parallel mineralized veins in this vicinity remaining to be discovered.

Despite more than 150 years of active collecting at this locality, the prospects for future collecting are excellent. Some of the best specimens preserved from these sites were collected in the past ten years and there is still much area yet to be explored that may be richly mineralized.

Geology and Origin

The geology of this locality is complex, and its interpretation is hindered by limited exposures of outcrop. The basic rock types present include the Grenville Marble and locally gneissic skarn-like assemblages of tourmaline, diopside, phlogopite, and quartz, with or without pyrite. Well-formed crystals of these same minerals tend to occur in contact with coarse-grained calcite that forms pods or veins in the host rock. Feldspars are conspicuously absent.

The tourmaline mineralization almost certainly formed during the widespread regional metamorphism of the Adirondack Lowlands in the late Precambrian. The source of boron for the large amount of tourmaline at this occurrence was most likely one or more evaporite layers in the original Precambrian sedimentary sequence that was metamorphosed. The minerals on top of the hill are hosted by marble and a complex variety of metasediments. The stream-side veins fill brittle fractures in metasedimentary gneisses. The mineralization in the southeastern area is largely still covered, and its detailed geological relationships remain unclear.

Tourmaline, quartz, phlogopite, diopside, fluorapatite, and calcite probably formed as prograde minerals during regional metamorphism, while talc, chlorite, vermiculite, and tremolite formed as retrograde minerals toward the end of regional metamorphism. At least one phase of later hydrothermal mineralization occurred sometime in the Paleozoic after the calcite cores of the stream-side veins had partially weathered away, depositing quartz, calcite, microcline, pyrite, sphalerite, chalcopyrite, chamosite, talc, and the rare-earth minerals allanite-(Ce) and synchysite-(Ce). Calcite and chalcopyrite were also deposited in open fractures in the smoky quartz vein on top of the hill.

Minerals

Studies on this locality are ongoing and a complete list of minerals does not yet exist. The most important minerals for collectors are prograde metamorphic minerals, some of which have been altered by retrograde metamorphism. The later hydrothermal minerals filling fractures are usually of greatest interest to micromounters. Pseudomorphs of various minerals are widespread at this locality and are therefore listed separately.

Actinolite, $Ca_2(Mg,Fe^{2+})_5Si_8O_{22}(OH)_2$, occurs as prismatic lustrous black crystals to 10 cm on top of the hill.

Allanite-(Ce), $CaCeFe^{2+}Al_2(Si_2O_7)(SiO_4)O(OH)$, is a late-stage mineral that occurs as black acicular crystals to several millimeters on top of the hill and as submicroscopic prismatic crystals in the phosphate vein.

Calcite, $CaCO_3$, occurs most commonly as the matrix of other prograde metamorphic minerals, but also as late-stage rhombohedral crystals to several centimeters in the smoky quartz vein and to several millimeters in the phosphate vein.

Chalcopyrite, $CuFeS_2$, occurs as a late-stage hydrothermal mineral on top of the hill in dark brown bisphenoids to a centimeter, especially in the smoky quartz vein, and as iridescent bisphenoids to several millimeters in the phosphate vein.

Chamosite, $(Fe,Al,Mg)_6(Si, Al)_4O_{10}(OH)_8$, occurs as a later-stage hydrothermal mineral in the phosphate vein, forming microscopic dark green rosettes associated with quartz and microcline.

Chlorite Group minerals occur as alteration products of phlogopite.

Diopside, $CaMgSi_2O_6$, occurs as prograde prismatic green crystals to 10 cm. Many are blocky with a square cross-section, but some have additional prism faces. Much of the diopside from this locality exhibits various stages of uralitization as a result of alteration during retrograde metamorphism.

Dravite, $(Na,Ca)Mg_3Al_6(BO_3)_3[Si_6O_{18}](OH,O)_4$, occurs as lustrous iron-rich black crystals to 10 cm and in clusters or crystals to 30 cm or more. Most of the crystals are equant and show no striations on the prism faces. An exception is some of the crystals from the Waddell vein. Hemimorphic crystals with a pointed end and a flattened end are relatively common. Determining the appropriate species name for these outstanding tourmaline crystals has an interesting history. Initially, because they were black, most of them were labeled as schorl. In 1977, Dunn and colleagues suggested labeling them iron-rich uvite. In the recent past, various authors have labeled them either uvite or dravite based upon how they interpreted their analyses. A recent unpublished study to investigate possible compositional trends across the various sites at the locality found very little variability in the major constituents. Using new analyses and the most recent nomenclature for the tourmaline group just published by Henry, *et al.*, Dr. Marian Lupulescu has determined that most black tourmaline at this locality is dravite, although its composition is fairly close to the dravite/uvite boundary. We suggest that these black tourmalines be labeled dravite unless an analysis shows otherwise for a specific specimen.

Fluorapatite, $Ca_5(PO4)_3F$, occurs as prograde, simple, gray-green, hexagonal prisms across the locality, although most crystals over 1 cm have a dull surface luster. An exception is the phosphate vein where transparent yellow crystals to 8 mm and lustrous green crystals to several centimeters, sometimes in clusters, have been found.

Goethite, FeO(OH), occurs as earthy brown masses, especially in the phosphate vein, middle vein, and Wallace-Carlin vein, where it formed as a weathering product of pyrite. Goethite also partially or completely replaces pyrite crystals across the locality.

Gold, Au, has been observed as minute crystals to several microns in thin sections of prograde quartz from the phosphate trench.

Magnetite, Fe_3O_4, occurs rarely as lustrous black octahedral crystals to 1 cm associated with tremolite on top of the hill.

Fig. 94. Dravite. Powers Farm, Pierrepont, St. Lawrence Co. 5 cm. Jay Walter collection. MW

Fig. 95. Dravite. Waddell Trench, Powers Farm, Pierrepont, St. Lawrence Co. 5.8 cm. Steven C. Chamberlain collection. MW

Malachite, $Cu_2^{2+}(CO_3)(OH)_2$, is a frequent green alteration product coating chalcopyrite crystals, especially in the smoky quartz vein on the top of the hill.

Marcasite, FeS_2, occurs as a late-stage hydrothermal mineral in large hemispherical masses of radiating crystals to 5 cm in the Wallace-Carlin vein and as individual crystals to several millimeters in the phosphate vein.

Microcline, $KAlSi_3O_8$, occurs as a late-stage hydrothermal mineral in the phosphate vein as microscopic white crystals associated with chamosite and quartz.

Phlogopite, $KMg_3AlSi_3O_{10}(OH)_2$, forms prograde dark brown, iron-rich, pseudohexagonal crystals that taper on both ends. Good specimens have especially been found on top of the hill and in the phosphate vein.

Pyrite, FeS_2, occurs as prograde masses and cubic crystals to 1 cm or more, often somewhat altered to goethite across the locality. Brilliant brassy crystals with complex crystal forms occur as a late-stage hydrothermal mineral in the phosphate trench.

Quartz, SiO_2, occurs as tapered, Tessin-habit prisms to 10 cm or more across the locality. These prograde quartz crystals are usually translucent, white to tan, or pale smoky striated prisms. Colorless quartz that formed as a late-stage hydrothermal mineral occurs in the Waddell and phosphate veins as brilliant terminated prisms. Lustrous smoky quartz crystals ranging from pale tan to almost black occur in the smoky quartz vein in prisms to 10 cm and in clusters to 20 cm or more, sometimes associated with dravite-uvite and rhombohedral calcite crystals.

Sphalerite, ZnS, occurs rarely as a late-stage hydrothermal mineral forming lustrous yellow crystals to several millimeters in the phosphate vein.

Scapolite Group minerals occur as creamy white prisms to 6 cm, but are more commonly partially or wholly altered to other minerals as pseudomorphs.

Synchysite-(Ce), $Ca(Ce,La)(CO_3)_2F$, is a late-stage hydrothermal mineral, forming microscopic, lath-like, or tabular pseudohexagonal crystals in fractures in dravite in the phosphate vein,

Fig. 96. Dravite. Powers Farm, Pierrepont, St. Lawrence Co. 5 cm. A. E. Seaman Mineral Museum. GWR

Fig. 97. Dravite, quartz. Powers Farm, Pierrepont, St. Lawrence Co. 12 cm fov. Canadian Museum of Nature. JAS

Talc, $Mg_3Si_4O_{10}(OH)_2$, occurs as a coating on quartz and retrograde alteration of diopside and scapolite across the locality. Late-stage hydrothermal crystals of talc to several millimeters occur in the Waddell vein and phosphate veins.

Tremolite, $Ca_2Mg_5Si_8O_{22}(OH)_2$, is a common retrograde mineral across the locality in crystals to several centimeters and clusters of crystals to 10 cm. In color, the tremolite ranges from light green to dark green, almost black, and dark brown. Not all of these color variants have been analyzed. Tremolite is also one of several minerals replacing and overgrowing diopside crystals.

Vermiculite, $(Mg,Fe,Al)_3((Al,Si)_4O_{10})(OH)_2 \cdot 4H_2O$, occurs as a brown alteration product replacing phlogopite crystals in the phosphate vein and on top of the hill.

Pseudomorphs

Chlorite after phlogopite occurs as green submetallic zones in phlogopite crystals, especially on top of the hill and in the middle vein.

Goethite after pyrite occurs as brown masses and cubic crystals with residual pyrite cores that have formed by weathering.

Pyrite after quartz occurs on top of the hill as replacements of tapered quartz crystals to several centimeters.

Quartz after diopside occurs as white replacements of blocky diopside crystals on top of the hill and at the southeastern area. Occasionally a single diopside crystal will be replaced by quartz on one end and by tremolite on the other. In the phosphate vein, prismatic diopside crystals have been replaced with translucent gray quartz.

Quartz after phlogopite occurs as exfoliated crystals to 8 cm in the phosphate vein. These are unusual and appear to have formed after the embedding calcite had weathered away to allow for the attendant volume changes required. The phlogopite was probably first replaced by chlorite, which requires expansion, and subsequently, the exfoliated lamellae were wholly replaced by translucent gray quartz, with late-stage hydrothermal quartz crystals forming in the spaces between the folia.

Talc after diopside occurs as dull green blocky crystals to 8 cm on top of the hill. Frequently talc is mixed with other minerals in these pseudomorphs.

Fig. 98. *Dravite. Wallace-Carlin Trench, Powers Farm, Pierrepont, St. Lawrence Co. 8 cm. Steven C. Chamberlain collection. SCC*

Fig. 99. *Dravite. Powers Farm, Pierrepont, St. Lawrence Co. 4.1 cm. Michael Walter collection. MW*

Talc after quartz occurs as thick encrustations and partial to complete replacements of tapered Tessin-habit quartz crystals on top of the hill and in the phosphate vein.

Talc after scapolite occurs as translucent green crystals to 5 cm on top of the hill. Dark green to black altered scapolite crystals from the phosphate and Waddell veins probably contain a mixture of talc and other minerals.

Vermiculite after phlogopite occurs as brown submetallic zones in phlogopite crystals in the phosphate trench.

Similar Occurrences

There are numerous localities for various tourmaline species in the Adirondack Lowlands that were probably formed when boron-containing evaporites in the Precambrian sedimentary layers were regionally metamorphosed in late Precambrian time. However, none of them is particularly similar to the Pierrepont black tourmaline occurrence in terms of its overall geology, quality, and quantity of tourmaline crystals, or large number of collectible accessory minerals.

Fig. 101. Quartz. Powers Farm, Pierrepont, St. Lawrence Co. 5.8 cm. Steven C. Chamberlain collection. SCC

Fig. 100. Quartz. Powers Farm, Pierrepont, St. Lawrence Co. 11 cm. Steven C. Chamberlain collection. SCC

References

AGAR, W. M. (1921) The minerals of St. Lawrence, Jefferson, and Lewis Counties, NY. *American Mineralogist* 6:148-153, 158-164.

AGAR, W. M. (1923) Contact metamorphism in the western Adirondacks. *Proceedings of the American Philosophical Society* 62:95-174.

CHAMBERLAIN, S. C. (2007) Excavation of a pegmatite dike on the Bower Powers farm, Pierrepont, St. Lawrence County, New York. *Rocks & Minerals* 82:233-234.

CHAMBERLAIN, S. C., BAILEY, D. G., and WALTER, M., (2010) Minerals of the phosphate vein, Bower Powers farm, Pierrepont, St. Lawrence County, New York. *Rocks & Minerals* 85:162-163.

CROSS, R. T. (1903) *Crystals and Gold*. The Nebraska Newspaper Union, York, Nebraska. 196p.

DUNN, P. J., APPLEMAN, D., NELEN, J. A., and NORBERG, J. (1977) Uvite, a new (old) common member of the tourmaline group and its implication for collectors. *Mineralogical Record* 8:100-108.

FISH, D. S. (1982) The history, geology, mineralogy, and paragenesis of the black tourmaline locality, Pierrepont, New York. Bachelor's Thesis, Hamilton College. 56p.

HENRY, D. J., NOVAK, M., HAWTHORNE, F. C., ERTL, A., DUTROW, B. L., UHER, P., and PEZZOTTA, F. (2011) Nomenclature of the tourmaline-supergroup minerals. *American Mineralogist* 96:895-913.

HOUGH, F. B. (1853) *History of St. Lawrence and Franklin Counties, New York*. Little & Co., Albany. 719p.

ROBINSON, G. W. and ALVERSON, S. (1971) *Minerals of the St. Lawrence Valley*. Privately published. 42p.

WALTER, M. (2000) Uvites you can dig. *Rock & Gem* 30(11):56-59.

WALTER, M. (2007) *Field Collecting Minerals in the Empire State*. Privately published. 212p.

WALTER, M. R. and CHAMBERLAIN, S. C. (2010) History of the Powers Farm streamside veins, St. Lawrence County, New York. *Rocks & Minerals* 85:556.

YAU, Y-C., ANOVITZ, L. M., ESSENE, E. J., and PEACOR, D. R. (1984) Phlogopite-chlorite reaction mechanisms and physical conditions during retrograde reactions in the Marble Formation, Franklin, New Jersey. *Contributions to Mineralogy and Petrology* 88:299-306.

Fig. 102. Talc, quartz, dravite. Waddell Trench, Powers Farm, Pierrepont, St. Lawrence Co. 7 cm. Steven C. Chamberlain collection. MW

Fig. 103. "Uralite," calcite. Powers Farm, Pierrepont, St. Lawrence Co. 5.6 cm. Steven C. Chamberlain collection. MW

Overlook Quarry

Significance

The Overlook quarry was commercially operated for feldspar, but is much better known for its large crystals of black tourmaline (schorl) and the rare species, polycrase-(Y). Not only do some of the schorl crystals rank among the finest large crystals found anywhere in the United States, but they also have special historic importance as they comprised a significant portion of the tourmaline used to make pressure gauges used by the Allied Forces in World War II.

Location and History

The Overlook quarry is in Saratoga County about 5 miles southwest of the village of Hadley at 43°17'42"N, 73°56'11"W. It is also known as the Atlas, Day, or York quarry, or "quarry near Linwood School." We could find no reference as to when quarrying began, but in his 1923 *Geology of the Luzerne Quadrangle*, Miller states that operations ceased in the spring of 1920. In the 1930s and 1940s, Elmer Rowley made many trips by bicycle from his home in Glens Falls in order to collect crystal sections of tourmaline that were sold in Great Britain to make pressure gauges. The larger, more perfect crystals were kept, and are now in the collection of the New York State Museum. Similar crystals, though fewer in number, were sporadically found through the 1950s and '60s by other Glens Falls mineral collectors, Ralph Lapham, Robert Swigert, and George Robinson. Today the quarry is completely filled in and the land reclaimed so that collecting is very limited.

Geology and Origin

The Overlook pegmatite is of Grenvillian age and in the modern-day nomenclature proposed by Cerny, would be classed as a Rare-Element NYF-type pegmatite (NYF = niobium-yttrium-fluorine). According to Tan's 1966 monograph on New York pegmatites, the Overlook pegmatite is zoned with a fine-grained border/wall zone in sharp contact with the granitic gneiss and metagabbro country rocks. In areas, foliated sheets of biotite approaching 1.2 m across were observed. The intermediate zone contained large crystals of microcline 0.3–1 m across and 15 to 25 cm long schorl crystals. In the 1950s, a small portion of the smoky and rose quartz core was still visible in the north end of the quarry, where sharp molds once occupied by terminated schorl crystals nearly 30 cm long and 10 cm in diameter were clearly visible.

Minerals

Of the dozen or more minerals reported from this locality only four are of primary interest to mineral collectors: monazite-(Ce), rose quartz, schorl, and uranopolycrase. The others, for the most part, occur as subhedral to anhedral crystals or grains frozen in pegmatite matrix.

Monazite-(Ce), $(Ce,La,Nd)PO_4$, is not common at this locality, though when found, may occur in well-formed resinous brown crystals to more than 3 cm across.

Quartz, SiO_2, is common in all granitic pegmatites. While no well-formed crystals were ever found at the Overlook quarry, the massive quartz core provided hundreds of pounds of bright pink rose quartz popular with both mineral collectors and lapidaries.

Fig. 104. Schorl, quartz. Overlook Quarry, Saratoga Co. 15.5 cm. Steven C. Chamberlain collection. SCC

Schorl, $Na(Fe^{2+})_3Al_6(BO_3)_3[Si_6O_{18}](OH)_4$, is undoubtedly the mineral for which this locality is most famous. Well-formed crystals from 2 to nearly 30 cm in length were once relatively abundant as elongated trigonal prisms with simple shallow rhombohedral terminations. Although the sharpest crystals were most often found frozen in quartz, they tended to break free from their enclosing matrix with little to no damage. Crystal sections to 20 cm in diameter have been reported, but the finest specimens are those 2–8 cm in diameter and 7–25 cm in length. Because of the natural tendency for the quartz to shatter away from the crystals, matrix specimens of schorl are relatively uncommon.

Uranopolycrase, $(U,Y)(Ti,Nb)_2O_6$, is a relatively rare mineral that occurs in certain NYF-type pegmatites.

At the Overlook quarry, it forms tabular pinacoidal crystals up to 2.5 cm long, frozen in quartz-microcline-biotite matrix. Their interiors typically appear a glassy brownish black as compared to their somewhat altered greenish brown exteriors. In the 1950s, they were found throughout the dump material and *in situ* along the back wall of the quarry near large books of biotite.

Similar Occurrences

Greenfield chrysoberyl locality (43°01'30"N, 73°46'53"W); Clapska Mining Co. property near Batchellerville (43°14'23"N, 74°03'03"W); Roe spar bed, Crown Point (43°58'55"N, 73°32'24"W).

Fig. 105. *Schorl. Overlook Quarry, Saratoga Co. 8.4 cm. New York State Museum. ML*

Fig. 106. *Uranopolycrase. Overlook Quarry, Saratoga Co. 2.5 cm crystal. New York State Museum. ML*

References

CERNY, P. (1991) Rare-element granite pegmatites. I. Anatomy and internal evolution of pegmatite deposits. *Geoscience Canada*, 18:49-67.

FRONDEL, C. (1948) Tourmaline pressure gauges. *American Mineralogist* 33:1-17.

LUPULESCU, M. (2007) Minerals from New York State pegmatites. *Rocks & Minerals* 82:494-500.

MILLER, W. J. (1923) Geology of the Luzerne Quadrangle. *New York State Museum Bulletin No. 246.*

ROWLEY, E. B. (1942) Huge tourmaline crystals discovered. *The Mineralogist* 10:42-48, 63-64.

ROWLEY, E. B. (1960) Monazite and cyrtolite at Day, New York pegmatite. *Rocks & Minerals* 35:328-330.

SMITH, E. S. C. and KRUESI, O. (1942) Polycrase in New York State. *American Mineralogist* 32:585-587.

TAN, L.-P. (1966) Major pegmatite deposits of New York State. *New York State Museum and Science Service Bulletin 408.*

Bedford Pegmatites

Significance

This group of pegmatites produced fine specimens of schorl, columbite, microcline, almandine, quartz, ilmenite, and beryl among numerous other mineral species.

Location and History

A number of pegmatite bodies, mined mostly for feldspar, are located in a small area immediately southeast of the village of Bedford in Westchester County. The Kinkel quarry (41°11'50"N, 73°38'01"W) was first opened in 1875 and was followed by the Hobby quarry (41°10'45"N, 73°36'54"W), the Buresch quarry (41°11'35"N, 73°37'59"W), the Baylis and Speranza quarries (41°11'46"N, 73°38'21"W), and several others (Bullock quarry, Clinchfield quarry, Colgate quarry, Kelt quarry, MacDonald quarry). By 1949, all mining activity in the area had stopped. By 1963, the dumps and mining structures of the Kinkel quarry had been leveled and graded for the construction of homes. Of these, the Kinkel and Baylis quarries appear to have produced the largest number of high-quality specimens. Many collectors gained access while these quarries were operating, including through field trips of the New York Mineralogical Club.

The high-quality feldspar produced from Bedford pegmatites was designated by the commercial name, Lenox Spar, and was used by Lenox, Inc. to produce fine china. The Kinkel quarry provided the feldspar for the first set of White House china made in the United States.

This 1918 Woodrow Wilson china remained in service until the end of the Herbert Hoover administration.

Geology and Origin

The Bedford pegmatites are complex, zoned, granitic pegmatites that were emplaced in rocks of Taconic age (450 Ma) during the time interval from 380 to 360 Ma. None of them shows any trace of subsequent metamorphism.

Minerals

There has been no modern study of the minerals from this locality, and some of the identifications may be tentative. Minerals reported to occur include: albite (cleavelandite), allanite, almandine, apatite, autunite, beryl (aquamarine, heliodor), bertrandite, biotite, bismuthinite, bismutite, columbite-(Fe), epistilbite, galena, goethite, graphite, hematite, ilmenite, kaolinite, magnetite, microcline, muscovite, opal (hyalite), phosphuranylite, pyrite, pyrolusite, pyroxene, quartz (smoky, rose, citrine), rutile, schorl, titanite, torbernite, uraninite, uranophane, and zircon (cyrtolite). Only those species providing high-quality specimens are described below.

Almandine, $Fe_3Al_2(SiO_4)_3$, occurs as lustrous, trapezohedral, dark reddish brown to black crystals to 8 cm.

Beryl, $Be_3Al_2Si_6O_{18}$, occurs as green or yellow hexagonal crystals to 90 cm long and almost as large in diameter. Smaller crystals with a diameter of several centimeters often taper almost to a point. Most beryl crystals are opaque and many are stained red or brown by iron. Rarely, material suitable for faceting was found.

Columbite-(Fe), $FeNb_2O_6$, occurs as black, submetallic crystals to 24 cm. The best specimens have brilliant black crystal faces, but many have faces with lower luster.

Ilmenite, $FeTiO_3$, occurs as sharp, black, platy crystals to 10 cm embedded in smoky or citrine quartz or between schorl crystals and their milky quartz matrix.

Microcline, $KAlSi_3O_8$, is the most common feldspar and occurs in huge pink crystals that weigh several hundred pounds. Baveno twins are common.

Quartz, SiO_2, occurs in crystals, often in cavities completely surrounded by feldspar. Colorless, white, smoky, and citrine crystals have been found. Some quartz crystals are doubly terminated with textbook development of faces; others are flattened or bent. Smoky quartz crystals are often very transparent and glassy. Massive, translucent, rose quartz from this locality is often asteriated and shows a six, twelve, eighteen, or twenty-four-rayed star when cut into cabochons or spheres.

Fig. 107. Columbite-(Fe). Bedford, Westchester Co. 9 cm. New York State Museum. GBG

Schorl, $Na(Fe)_3Al_6(BO_3)_3[Si_6O_{18}](OH)_4$, occurs as lustrous, black, prismatic crystals. When doubly terminated, they show hemimorphic development of terminal faces. Larger crystals to 46 cm tend to have striated prism faces. Green tourmaline has been reported, but seemingly never analyzed to determine which species it is.

Zircon, $ZrSiO_4$, occurs as chocolate-brown, somewhat curved, tetragonal crystals to several cm. They are the variety "cyrtolite," and are enriched in both uranium and hafnium.

Similar Occurrences

Clapska Mining Company quarry, Batchellerville (43°14'21"N, 74°03'33"W); Overlook quarry, Overlook (43°17'30"N, 73°56'45"W); Kensico Dam quarry, Valhalla (41°04'15"N, 73°45'14"W).

Fig. 108. Microcline. Kinkel Quarry, Bedford, Westchester Co. 16.5 cm. Hudson River Museum. ER

Fig. 109. Muscovite, quartz. Bedford, Westchester Co. 6 cm. Steven C. Chamberlain collection. SCC

References

BLACK, D. (1948) Some minerals of Bedford, N. Y. *Rocks & Minerals* 23:710-712.

JENSEN, D. E. (1978) *Minerals of New York State*. Ward Press, Rochester. 219p.

LUPULESCU, M. (2007) Minerals from New York State, pegmatites. *Rocks & Minerals* 82:494-500.

MANCHESTER, J. G. (1931a) The minerals of New York City and its environs. *Bulletin of the New York Mineralogical Club* 3, 168p + plates.

MANCHESTER, J. G. (1931b) The metropolitan mineral area of New York City. *Rocks & Minerals* 6:114-125.

POUGH, F. H. (1936) Bertrandite and epistilbite from Bedford, New York. *American Mineralogist* 21:264-265.

TAN, L.-P. (1966) Major pegmatite deposits of New York State. *New York State Museum and Science Service Bulletin 408.*

WEIDHAAS, E. (1959) The large Bedford tourmaline group. *Rocks & Minerals* 34:390-392.

ZODAC, P. (1935) Ilmenite at Bedford, N. Y. *Rocks & Minerals* 10:86-87.

Greenfield Chrysoberyl Locality

Significance

Having been known for over 200 years, the Greenfield chrysoberyl locality is among the earliest of U. S. mineral localities. While not of gem quality or large size, chrysoberyl crystals from this locality are considered as "classics" and may be seen in major mineral museums worldwide.

Location and History

Located about a mile north of Saratoga Springs, in the Town of Greenfield, Saratoga County, at 43°01'30"N, 73°46'53"W, this chrysoberyl occurrence is one of the earliest discovered important mineral localities in the United States. The date of its discovery has often been inferred as 1821, based on a letter written by John Steel to Benjamin Silliman that year, but records in the British Museum (Natural History) show that a specimen of chrysoberyl from Greenfield was presented to the museum by Archibald Bruce in 1811, proving its existence was known at least a decade earlier.

Probably the most productive collecting was carried out in the mid-1800s, and the locality remained largely forgotten until it was rediscovered by Union College geologists Robert Navias and John Ostrom circa 1950.

Over the next decade, the site was visited by Elmer Rowley and other Glens Falls and Albany area collectors, all of whom found a number of small crystals by breaking up larger pieces of pegmatite in the rubble adjacent to the workings. In 1963, George Robinson and Michael Hubinsky completely excavated the old trench and screened what was left of the original dumps. About a dozen reasonably good specimens were recovered, including an unusual tapered crystal approximately 4 cm long, now in the collection of the Canadian Museum of Nature, Ottawa, Ontario. Perhaps the most recent serious collecting was done by Clifford Stevens in the early 1980s, who is reported to have found "many small crystals (up to 1.5 cm) displaying the typical wedge-shaped twin habit." Today the locality is on private property, and collecting is not allowed.

Geology and Origin

The occurrence itself consists of a small dike or lens of granitic pegmatite enclosed in Precambrian, Grenville-age gneiss, and is exposed by a trench from 2–8 feet deep along its strike. The pegmatite shows no obvious relationship to any granitic intrusion, and may have resulted from partial *in situ* melting during high-grade metamorphism (an anatectic pegmatite). It is mineralogically simple, consisting of quartz, microcline, and mica with minor amounts of schorl, almandine, sillimanite, and chrysoberyl, which further hinders its classification into one of the generally accepted genetic classes of granitic pegmatites.

Fig. 110. Chrysoberyl. Greenfield, Saratoga Co. 1 cm crystal. New York State Museum. SN

Minerals

In addition to the minerals listed above, the only others reported from this locality are apatite, beryl, and columbite, none of which can be confirmed. While they are colorful, the reddish almandine crystals are generally small (less than 0.6 cm) and subhedral; the black prisms of schorl are seldom longer than 1.3 cm and rarely show terminations; and only rarely are 2.5 cm crystals of pale tan microcline seen, leaving chrysoberyl as the locality's only species of collector interest.

Chrysoberyl, $BeAl_2O_4$, occurs as pale yellowish green crystals scattered throughout the pegmatite. Most show cyclic twinning, forming tabular, pseudohexagonal crystals to 3 cm in diameter, though most are less than half that size. Untwinned crystals are rare. While glassy, most crystals appear translucent to nearly opaque, with no transparent, gem-quality crystals having ever been found.

Similar Occurrences

Pegmatite found in 1893 at 88th Street and Amsterdam Avenue, New York City (40°47'28"N, 73°58'25"W); pegmatite found in 1901 at 93rd Street and Riverside Park, New York City (40°47'21"N, 73°58'08"W); prospect pit on former Clapska Mining Co. property near Batchellerville (43°14'21"N, 74°03'33"W).

References

BRITISH MUSEUM (1904) *The History of the Collections Contained in the Natural History Departments of the British Museum* 1:360-417. Printed by the Order of the Trustees of the British Museum, London.

KOIVULA, J. I. (1984) Gem News: New York Chrysoberyl. *Gems and Gemology* 20:121-122.

LEVISON, W. G. (1901a) Note on a Chrysoberyl From the Borough of Manhattan, New York City. *The Mineral Collector* 8:80-83.

LEVISON, W. G. (1901b) A Crystal of Chrysoberyl from Ninety-Third Street and Riverside Park. *The Mineral Collector* 8:134-136.

LUPULESCU, M. (2010) *Pegmatites of New York. Program Notes, 37th Rochester Mineralogical Symposium,* Rochester Academy of Science, Rochester, NY 18-22.

NAVAIS, R. A. and OSTROM, J. H. (1951) The Occurrence of Chrysoberyl at Greenfield, New York. *American Journal of Science* 249:308–311.

STEEL, J. H. (1822) Communication. *American Journal of Science and Arts,* Series 1, 4:37–38.

Fig. 112. *Microcline. Greenfield, Saratoga Co. 7 cm. Steven C. Chamberlain collection. SCC*

Fig. 111. *Chrysoberyl. Greenfield, Saratoga Co. 1.5 cm. Canadian Museum of Nature. SN*

Chapter 4
Occurrences in Fractures

This chapter presents detailed accounts of seven localities where crystallized minerals of interest to collectors have formed in veins or fractures. Some of these are well known classic historic localities: the Rossie lead mines, the Sterling iron mine, the Ellenville lead (zinc) mine, the Chub Lake hematite prospect, and the Muscalonge Lake and Macomb fluorite occurrences. Others are more modern occurrences: the zinc mines of the Balmat-Edwards mining district, and the Yellow Lake road cut.

Rossie Lead Mines

Significance

The Rossie lead mines are a classic early American mineral locality famous for their large, complex, often twinned crystals of calcite (Iceland spar) as well as large, cubic crystals of galena, specimens of which are preserved in most of the world's major mineral museums. Recent studies have identified a widespread group of similar, genetically related deposits across northern New York State and adjoining southeastern Ontario.

Location and History

There are a number of small mines and prospects that make up the Rossie lead mines, the largest and most important of which are the Coal Hill, Union, and Victoria veins, located approximately 1.5 miles south-southwest of the village of Rossie in St. Lawrence County at (44°21'14"N, 75°39'57"W), (44°21'34"N, 75°39'18"W), and (44°21'57"N, 75°39'12"W) respectively. These veins were discovered in the 1830s and worked for lead by several small, local mining companies through the 1850s, with the last activity recorded in 1876, and an estimated 6,000 tons of lead having been produced. Lewis Beck gave a contemporary account of the mines and minerals when he visited the Coal Hill vein in August, 1836:

The average width of the vein was two feet, and it cut the rock in a nearly perpendicular direction … its length, as exposed at that time was about four hundred and fifty feet … the galena found in this vein is often crystallized in large cubes … Throughout the whole extent of the vein, the ore is imbedded in a gangue of carbonate of lime, with druses of calcareous spar of great beauty, and presenting a great variety of crystalline forms … Fine druses of crystallized galena and calcareous spar, together with variously modified crystals of iron pyrites and some copper pyrites, were from time to time laid open. A few beautiful specimens of crystallized sulphate of strontian [celestine] of a bluish color were also found. (Beck 1842, 48–49)

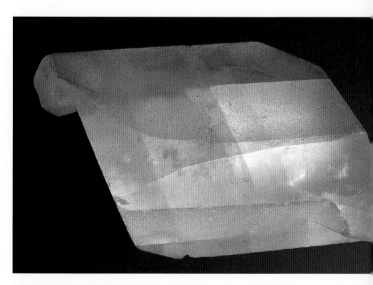

Fig. 113. Calcite. Rossie Lead Mines, Rossie, St. Lawrence Co. 19 cm. Root collection, New York State Museum. SCC

In 1950, the Coal Hill and Union veins were diamond-drilled by the U. S. Bureau of Mines in search of lead and zinc reserves but with discouraging results. Except for a large chimney still standing at the Victoria vein and a few water-filled shafts sunk on the Coal Hill and Union veins, little remains of the mines today. All are on private lands, though permission to visit them is sometimes granted.

Geology and Origin

The origin of the Rossie calcite-galena veins has been debated since their discovery. The three principal veins discussed above cut Grenville-age gneissic granite-granodiorite, and similar, but smaller, nearby veins cut the overlying Cambrian-age Potsdam Sandstone, as well as Ordovician-age limestone in areas to the northwest in southeastern Ontario, clearly establishing their age as post-Ordovician. Radiometric $^{40}Ar/^{39}Ar$ dating of microcline (adularia) from the Coal Hill vein gives an age of 186 million years, and combined trace element, stable isotope, and fluid inclusion studies suggest the veins resulted from downward-moving fluids that leached lead and other elements from the Grenvillian host rocks forming relatively low-temperature hydrothermal solutions that subsequently mineralized gash veins and faults that had probably formed during the earlier Acadian orogeny. These same hydrothermal solutions also reacted with the granitic wall rocks and xenoliths in some of the veins (e.g. Coal Hill) to form an alpine-like assemblage of minerals characterized by the presence of anatase, cerium-rich epidote, and synchysite-(Ce).

Fig. 114. Calcite. Rossie Lead Mines, Rossie, St. Lawrence Co. 14 cm. Root collection, New York State Museum. SN

Fig. 116. Calcite. Rossie Lead Mines, Rossie, St. Lawrence Co. 19 cm. ER

Fig. 115. Calcite. Rossie Lead Mines, Rossie, St. Lawrence Co. 15 cm. New York State Museum. SCC

Fig. 117. Galena. Rossie Lead Mines, Rossie, St. Lawrence Co. 8 cm. Canadian Museum of Nature. GWR

Minerals

The large calcite and galena crystals produced from the 1830s to 1850s are undoubtedly the two species for which the Rossie lead mines are best known, though good specimens of celestine, chalcopyrite, fluorite, marcasite, pyrite, and sphalerite were also recovered, but in fewer numbers. Supergene weathering products (e.g. anglesite, brochantite, cerussite, etc.) coat some of the sulfide minerals, but do not occur as collector-quality specimens. The recently discovered alpine suite of minerals includes small crystals of albite, anatase, cerium-rich epidote, microcline, quartz, and synchysite-(Ce), combinations of which can make interesting micromounts.

Albite, $NaAlSi_3O_8$, occurs as tabular, glassy crystals to 3 mm across associated with quartz and other species in the alpine suite, lining fractures and surfaces of altered granitic xenoliths.

Anatase, TiO_2, forms electric blue, tabular crystals to 0.5 mm associated with quartz and albite, coating surfaces and fractures in altered granitic xenoliths.

Calcite, $CaCO_3$, crystals from Rossie can be seen in mineral museums throughout the world. Their enormous size (up to 165 pounds), spectacular twinning, and complexity of forms and crystal habits were the focus of much interest by early mineralogists and crystallographers. Large rhombohedral crystals showing over a dozen modifying forms are known. Lewis Beck described the crystals in his 1842 *Mineralogy of New-York* as:

> Their forms are exceedingly various, and require various descriptions. Crystals of a delicate straw-yellow color, almost perfectly transparent, and from eight to ten inches in diameter have occasionally been found … They occur in water-filled cavities … and are associated with crystallized galena, iron and copper pyrites, and rarely crystallized celestine. (Beck 1842, 225)

Celestine, $SrSO_4$, occurs as tabular, gray-white to pale blue crystals to 3 cm on calcite, but good specimens are rare.

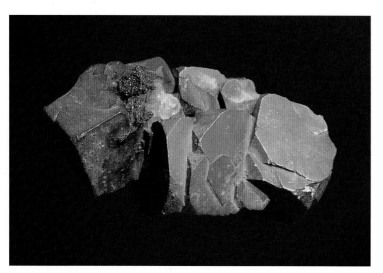

Fig. 118. Galena. Rossie Lead Mines, Rossie, St. Lawrence Co. 14 cm. Root collection, New York State Museum. SCC

Fig. 119. Pyrite. Rossie Lead Mines, Rossie, St. Lawrence Co. 3.5 cm. New York State Museum. SCC

Chalcopyrite, $CuFeS_2$, is occasionally seen as sharp, disphenoidal crystals to 0.5 mm scattered on the surfaces or as inclusions in some crystals of calcite.

Fluorite, CaF_2, is relatively uncommon, and most often occurs as simple green octahedral crystals to 1.5 cm on calcite crystals. Rarely, hexoctahedral overgrowths occur in perfect crystallographic alignment with the octahedrons, which also show dark purple, sector-zoned coloration along the *a* crystal axes, virtually identical to those from Old Chelsea, Québec.

Galena, PbS, occurs as simple cubes up to 15 cm across, often associated with calcite. Octahedron faces are common, while dodecahedron faces and spinel-law twins are uncommon. Groups of crystals weighing over 45 kg were found near the surface of the Coal Hill vein. Ebenezer Emmons described the occurrence in his 1842 geological report:

> Soon after the vein was opened, a large geode, or cavity termed a *water course* by miners was struck. This course was found lined with crystals of galena, whose edges ... were three inches in length. Some of the single crystals weighed 35 pounds; generally they came in groups, whose aggregate weight exceeded one hundred pounds. (Emmons 1842, 356)

Marcasite, FeS_2, is uncommon, but has been noted in both microscopic crystals with chalcopyrite and as botryoidal crusts coating calcite.

Microcline, $KAlSi_3O_8$, crystals are uncommon, but may form pale pink to flesh colored, bladed, adularia-habit crystals to 5 mm on calcite.

Pyrite, FeS_2, crystals are also uncommon, but when found can make very desirable specimens due to their crystallographic complexity. Lustrous, single crystals over 3 cm across showing various combinations of the cube, dodecahedron, octahedron, pyritohedron, trapezohedron, and diploid are known.

Sphalerite, ZnS, typically forms brown clots and stringers in the massive calcite vein, but occasionally resinous, yellow-brown crystals to 3 mm may occur scattered on crystallized calcite and galena.

Synchysite-(Ce), $Ca(Ce,La)(CO_3)_2F$, crystals occur in the alpine mineral assemblage as tabular, colorless to pale pink hexagonal crystals to 0.5 mm.

Similar Occurrences

Macomb lead mines (44°59'08"N, 75°32'34"W); Washburn farm copper mine (44°24'34"N, 75°31'54"W); Sterlingbush calcite cave (44°06'43"N, 75°29'43"W); Natural Bridge calcite locality (44°04'44"N, 75°29'50"W); Long Lake calcite-fluorite veins (44°02'42"N, 74°31'16"W); Yellow Lake (Laidlaw Lake) quartz locality (44°18'41"N, 75°36'51"W); Muscalonge Lake and Macomb fluorite occurrences (near 44°18'12"N, 75°41'12"W) and (44°23'26"N, 75°32'45"W), respectively.

References

AYUSO, R. A., FOLEY, N. K., and BROWN, C. E. (1987) Source of lead and mineralizing brines for Rossie-type Pb-Zn veins in the Frontenac Axis area, New York. *Economic Geology* 82:489-96.

BECK, L. C. (1842) *Mineralogy of New-York*. Thurlow Weed, Printer to the State, Albany, New York: p.212, p.244.

BROWN, C. E. (1983) Mineralization, mining, and mineral resources in the Beaver Creek area of the Grenville Lowlands in St. Lawrence County, New York. *U.S.G.S. Professional Paper 1279*:6, 13.

BUDDINGTON, A. F. (1934) Geology and mineral resources of the Hammond, Antwerp and Lowville quadrangles. *New York State Museum Bulletin* 296:202-227.

DIX, G. R. and ROBINSON, G.W. (2003) The geochemical record of hydrothermal mineralization and tectonism inboard of the Appalachian Orogen: the Ottawa Embayment. *Chemical Geology* 197:29-53.

EMMONS, E. (1842) *Geology of New-York, Part II. Comprising the Survey of the Second Geological District.* White and Visscher, Albany, New York: p. 354-60.

GRICE, J. D. (1981) Hexoctahedral fluorite crystals from Old Chelsea, Québec. *Mineralogical Record* 12:103-04.

HOUGH, F. B. (1853) *A History of St. Lawrence and Franklin Counties, New York.* Reprinted 1970, Regional Publishing Co., Baltimore, 455-467.

NASON, F. L. (1888) Some New York Minerals and Their Localities. *New York State Museum Bulletin No. 4.*

NEUMANN, G. L. (1952) Lead-Zinc deposits of southwestern St. Lawrence County, N.Y., *United States Bureau of Mines Report of Investigations 4907.*

RICHARDS, R. P., and ROBINSON, G. W. (2000) Mineralogy of the calcite-fluorite veins near Long Lake, New York, *Mineralogical Record* 31:413-422.

ROBINSON, G. W., DIX, G. R., CHAMBERLAIN, S. C., and HALL, C. (2001) Famous Mineral Localities: Rossie, New York, *Mineralogical Record* 32:273-293.

SMYTH, C. H., JR. (1903) The Rossie Lead Veins. *School of Mines Quarterly: Journal of Applied Science, Columbia University* 24:421-29.

WHITLOCK, H. P. (1910) Calcites of New York. *New York State Museum Memoir* 13:190p.

WHITLOCK, H. P. (1910) Fluorite, Rossie, St. Lawrence County. Contributions to *Mineralogy, New York State Bulletin* 140:198-99.

Muscalonge Lake and Macomb Fluorite Occurrences

Significance

Located approximately ten miles apart, these two early American mineral localities are famous for having produced pale green, lightly etched, cubic crystals of fluorite over 30 cm across. Specimens from these localities are today considered "classics" and can be seen in most of the world's major mineral museums, though specimens from Macomb are generally more common than those from Muscalonge Lake.

Location and History

The Muscalonge Lake locality (also spelled Muskellunge, Muscolunge, Muskalonge, among others) is the older of the two occurrences, having been discovered some forty years prior to the Macomb deposit. Lewis C. Beck described the Muscalonge Lake occurrence in his 1842 monograph, *Mineralogy of New-York*:

> One of the most remarkable localities for fluor spar in the United States is that which occurs on the southeast bank of Muscolunge Lake … The mineral is in a vein of considerable width, associated with calcareous spar, and running vertically or nearly so through a bed of primitive limestone [i.e. Grenville Marble]. Cubical crystals of various sizes have been found here, some of them more than a foot in diameter … it is now difficult to obtain good crystallized specimens, and there is some danger in working at the locality. (Beck 1842, 244)

Repeated attempts by numerous mineral collectors to relocate this vein have been unsuccessful, although a second, smaller occurrence also described by Beck as on the shoreline "a short distance north" of the main workings was rediscovered in the 1960s by Schuyler Alverson and George Robinson (near 44°18'12"N, 75°41'12"W), but only a handful of small cleavages of fluorite and calcite were found. Tiffany & Company's famous mineralogist/gemologist George F. Kunz described the locality as "a vein which ran under the lake," and some local residents believe that the main workings may now be below the lake level, which they claim has risen over the years.

Fortunately, the site of the Macomb fluorite mine is better known and is located on a hillside approximately 33 yards southeast of Rastley Road in the Town of Macomb, St. Lawrence County, near 44°23'26"N, 75°32'45"W. The locality was first discovered in 1885, and a contemporary description was given by George F. Kunz in 1889:

> … a small vein of fluorite in Archaen limestone [i.e. Grenville Marble] was discovered in the town of Macomb … [and] was worked from time to time until last summer, when the vein suddenly widened, breaking through into a cavity or cave. This cave is 22 feet north and south, and 18 feet east and west, and is 8 feet below the surface … The top, bottom, and sides were lined with a magnificent sheet of crystals, varying from one to six inches in diameter … Groups of crystals, weighing from ten to several hundred pounds each, and one of them measuring 2 × 3 feet, were easily detached. The cavity contained at least fifteen tons of fluorite. (Kunz 1889, 72–73)

Many of these large specimens were acquired by Kunz and sold to collectors and museums around the world. Apparently, little subsequent collecting was done, as the locality was probably assumed to be exhausted, and with time went from "forgotten" to "lost." In 1966, the site was rediscovered by Ray Putman, a local mineral collector, and soon thereafter visited by numerous others. Cleavages and partial crystals of pale green fluorite collected from the overgrown dump adjacent to a small water-filled pit left little doubt that this was indeed the famous "lost" Macomb fluorite locality. The following year a group of collectors (George Sechler, Carl Lashway, and George W. Robinson) dewatered the pit and entered the old workings in hope of finding more of the large cubic crystals for which the locality was known. At the bottom of the decline, they uncovered a 2 x 3 m long extension of the original "cave," but it contained only calcite. The group had better luck digging southwest along the strike of the vein, where they encountered a series of small pockets of disintegrated calcite containing large masses of fluorite and a single 15 cm cubic crystal.

No serious attempts to recover more specimens were made for the next quarter century until October, 1995, when landowner, Arthur Wilm, and neighbor, Jim Typher, decided to further excavate the vein in the same area as the 1967 party had dug. Encouraged by several showings of massive green fluorite attached to the hanging wall, they enlisted the assistance of William deLorraine and George Robinson for advice on how to remove the fluorite intact, which was easily accomplished using a portable drill and tongue-and-feather wedges. However, as experienced geologists and field collectors, Robinson and deLorraine were intrigued by some small groups of etched calcite crystals that had been found a few days earlier, and suggested it might be more profitable to continue digging where they had been found, as they were clearly indicative of an open pocket environment. Hence, attention was shifted to following a seam of crumbly calcite traversing the bottom of the hole, and in a short while, the seam widened into a pocket approximately 60 cm across, on the floor of which was a single 25 cm cube of green fluorite that was naturally detached from the wall and easily lifted out. It is likely that similar specimens lie in the unworked extensions of the vein, but to recover them will require a major mining effort, and collecting is not presently allowed.

Geology and Origin

The Muscalonge Lake and Macomb fluorite occurrences are geologically similar and consist of mineralized gash veins and infillings along water courses in Grenville Marble. Trace element and carbon isotope analyses of calcites from each occurrence are similar to those from the nearby Rossie lead mines (q.v.), suggesting they are genetically related to these deposits.

Minerals

Fluorite and calcite are the predominant species of interest at each of these localities. Small amounts of strontianite have been found at Muscalonge Lake, and minor chalcopyrite, pyrite, galena, sphalerite, and goethite have been reported from Macomb, but none as collector-quality specimens. Small, sparse crystals of pale green uvite-dravite have also been collected at the Macomb occurrence, but these are hosted by the Precambrian marble, and are genetically unrelated to the fluorite.

Fluorite, CaF_2, specimens from each of these two localities are virtually indistinguishable, save for occasional minor coatings of gray-white strontianite that have been observed on some of the fluorite from Muscalonge Lake. Otherwise, crystals from each locality tend to form simple, pale green, etched cubes from 2.5–30 cm on the edge. One large group of crystals from Macomb in the New York State Museum measures 48 × 66 cm.

Fig. 120. Fluorite. Muscalonge Lake, Jefferson Co. 12 cm. New York State Museum. ER

Fig. 122. Fluorite. Macomb, St. Lawrence Co. 8 cm. Steven C. Chamberlain collection, SCC

Fig. 121. Fluorite. Muscalonge Lake, Jefferson Co. 17 cm. A. E. Seaman Mineral Museum. GWR

Calcite, $CaCO_3$, crystals from the two occurrences are also similar in appearance, and typically form translucent, gray-white to pale yellow-white individuals that average 2.5–7.5 cm in length. The most commonly observed forms are combinations of the rhombohedron and scalenohedron in variable proportions, resulting in a range of habits; twinned crystals are not uncommon. Aggregates of such crystals are common at the Macomb locality, but unfortunately, crystal faces are nearly always etched or frosted due to dissolution by groundwater. The large pocket of calcite encountered in 1967 at the bottom of the decline was never excavated, and may contain better crystals, as they appeared to be covered by a protective layer of thick, white clay.

Similar Occurrences

Rossie lead mines (44°21'15"N, 75°39'54"W); Macomb lead mines (44°59'08"N, 75°32'34"W); Sterlingbush calcite cave (44°06'43"N, 75°29'43"W); Natural Bridge calcite locality (44°04'44"N, 75°29'50"W); Long Lake calcite-fluorite veins (44°02'42"N, 74°31'16"W); Yellow Lake (Laidlaw Lake) quartz locality (44°18'41"N, 75°36'51"W).

References

BECK, L. C. (1842) *Mineralogy of New-York*. Thurlow Weed, Printer to the State, Albany, New York. p. 212, p. 244.

BROWN, C. E. (1983) Mineralization, mining, and mineral resources in the Beaver Creek area of the Grenville Lowlands in St. Lawrence County, New York. *U.S.G.S. Professional Paper 1279*.

DIX, G. R. and ROBINSON, G.W. (2003) The geochemical record of hydrothermal mineralization and tectonism inboard of the Appalachian Orogen: the Ottawa Embayment. *Chemical Geology* 197:29-53.

KUNZ, G. F. (1889) Mineralogical notes, on fluorite, opal, amber and diamond. *American Journal of Science*, Series 3, 38:72-73.

KUNZ, G. F. (1892) *Gems and Precious Stones of North America*. Republished by Dover Publications, Inc., New York, NY, 1968. p. 183.

RICHARDS, R. P., and ROBINSON, G. W. (2000) Mineralogy of the calcite-fluorite veins near Long Lake, New York, *Mineralogical Record* 31:413-422.

ROBINSON, G. W., DIX, G. R., CHAMBERLAIN, S. C., and HALL, C. (2001) Famous Mineral Localities: Rossie, New York, *Mineralogical Record* 32:273-293.

Yellow Lake Road Cut

Significance

This locality is a good example of mineralization in a fracture zone exposed in a road cut where the source of the mineralizing fluids was local. Characteristic specimens of calcite crystals from this road cut are widely preserved in mineral collections.

Location and History

The Yellow Lake road cut is on the west side of St. Lawrence County Route 10 between its intersections with Robinson and Hall roads at 44°20'22"N, 75°36'14"W. For decades the center of collecting activity was toward the northern end of the exposed mineralized zone. In 2006, a new series of pockets was found about fifteen yards to the south. The two sites produced specimens that are distinctive and are often referred to as coming from Yellow Lake North and Yellow Lake South.

The locality appears to have be found during the widening of Route 10 in the early 1960s. George Robinson and Mike Hubinsky, then students at SUNY Potsdam, noted mineralized cavities late in the fall of 1964. In March, Robinson and his parents collected about 500 pounds of specimens and the next weekend Robinson and Hubinsky collected another 500 pounds. Shortly afterwards, John Pietras of Rome, NY, collected hundreds of high-quality specimens. Local collectors, Ivan McIntosh, Bob Johnson, and Charlie Bowman as well as many others subsequently collected at the site, which was listed as locality 19 in Robinson and Alverson's 1971 collecting guide.

Fig. 123. *Barite. Yellow Lake Road Cut, St. Lawrence Co. 25 cm. Michael Walter collection. MW*

In July 2006, Michael and Jay Walter discovered a new series of pockets farther south along the road cut that subsequently yielded many hundreds of high-quality specimens. At the end of several days' collecting, the excavated pockets were backfilled because they were in the berm of the highway.

Geology and Origin

The roadcut exposes Precambrian Grenville Marble that is part of an assemblage that also includes other metasedimentary and metavolcanic units. Tectonic activity produced fractures that allowed groundwater to form solution cavities and subsequently mineralize them. Pleistocene glaciation resulted in the filling of most of the large cavities with clay. The formation of the solution cavities and their subsequent mineralization reflect the changing composition of groundwaters over geologic time. The presence of quartz crystals with inclusions of graphite rosettes and fluor-uvite crystals from the overlying marble late in the mineralization sequence suggests the action of biologically-mediated mineralization. Organic acids entering the groundwater from the plants in the soil zone may hold silica from the weathering of metamorphic silicates (feldspars, scapolite) in solution until their eventual breakdown by bacteria causes quartz to precipitate.

Minerals

Although the color-zoned calcite crystals from this locality are best known, the barite and dolomite also make very attractive specimens.

Barite, $BaSO_4$, occurs as white to tan crystals to 18 cm and groups weighing more than 14 kg. Crystal faces are typically not smooth but have a frosted or feathery surface texture.

Calcite, $CaCO_3$, is the most significant mineral found at the locality. Crystals from the northern end of the road cut are typically untwinned scalenohedra $K\{21\bar{3}1\}$, terminated by smaller faces of the rhombohedron $p\{10\bar{1}1\}$. These usually have a dark brown core, a faint phantom outlined by microscopic pyrite or marcasite crystals, and a pale yellow zone at the termination. Individual crystals up to 15 cm form groups to 40 cm or larger. Crystals from the southern end of the road cut are occasionally scalenohedral, but more often show nearly equal development of the scalenohedron and rhombohedron and are sometimes twinned with contact plane $c(0001)$. These crystals lack the dark brown core, but frequently show the iron sulfide phantoms and zoned variation in color. The more equant calcite crystals occur to 12 cm and form groups to 30 cm.

Fig. 124. Calcite (twin). Yellow Lake Road Cut, St. Lawrence Co. 6 cm. Jay Walter collection. MW

Fig. 125. Calcite (twin). Yellow Lake Road Cut, St. Lawrence Co. 14 cm. Michael Walter collection. MW

Dolomite, $Ca(Mg,Fe)(CO_3)_2$, occurs as clusters of white to tan crystals to 5 cm, with individual crystals to 1 cm. It is paragenetically later than calcite and may be either epitactically or randomly oriented on the underlying calcite.

Fluor-uvite, $CaMg_3(MgAl_5)(BO_3)_3[Si_6O_{18}][F_3(OH)]$, occurs as green, yellow, and brown crystals and crystal fragments embedded in quartz. The original source of the fluor-uvite was the overlying marble.

Goethite, $FeO(OH)$, occurs as euhedral pseudomorphs after pyrite and marcasite and as anhedral coatings and stains.

Graphite, C, in flakes and rosettes to 1 mm occurs partially or wholly embedded in quartz. The original source of the graphite was the overlying marble.

Marcasite, FeS_2, as acicular and twinned crystals occurs as zones in calcite crystals.

Pyrite, FeS_2, forms crystalline plates to 11 cm with individual cuboctahedral crystals to 0.5 cm usually with some surface alteration to goethite.

Quartz, SiO_2, is a common late stage mineral in colorless crystals to several mm, often enclosing graphite and fluor-uvite crystals.

Similar Occurrences

Oxbow road cut (44°19'05"N, 75°37'54"W); Beaman Road barite locality (44°22'01"N, 75°29'10"W); Rock Island road cut (44°23'29"N, 75°27'14"W).

References

BENNETT, P. C. (1991) Quartz dissolution in organic-rich aqueous systems. *Geochimica et Cosmochimica Acta* 55:1781-1797.

BENNETT, P. and SIEGEL, D. I. (1987) Increased solubility of quartz in water due to complexing by organic compounds. *Nature* 326:684-686.

CHAMBERLAIN, S. C. and WALTER, M. (2006) Road-cut mineral occurrences of St. Lawrence County, New York. Part 2. Yellow Lake Road Cut. *Rocks & Minerals* 81:373.

ROBINSON, G. W. and ALVERSON, S. (1971) *Minerals of the St. Lawrence Valley*. Privately published. 42p.

WALTER, M. and CHAMBERLAIN, S. C. (2011) Road-cut mineral occurrences of St. Lawrence County, New York. Part 4. Yellow Lake South Road Cut. *Rocks & Minerals* 86:348-358.

Fig. 126. *Dolomite, calcite. Yellow Lake Road Cut, St. Lawrence Co. 12 cm. Michael Walter collection. MW*

Sterling Iron Mine

Significance

The Sterling iron mine was the first identified North American occurrence for the nickel sulfide, millerite, and is famous for having produced some of the world's finest specimens of this species. The locality has also been a source for attractive specimens of pecoraite, stilpnomelane, dolomite, siderite, hematite, and quartz.

Location and History

The Sterling mine is located approximately three miles north of the village of Antwerp, Jefferson County, at (44°14'18"N, 75°35'28"W) and is one of eleven old hematite mines that comprise the Antwerp-Keene belt. The property was generally considered as ordinary farmland until 1836 when it was acquired by the "Iron King of Northern New York," James Sterling, for the sum of $200. The Sterling Iron Company was formed the following year, and the first ore was hauled by horse-drawn wagons to a charcoal cold-air blast furnace at nearby Sterlingville, where it was wrought as pig iron. The mine remained in the Sterling family until 1869, when it was sold to the Jefferson Iron Company. In 1889, J. C. Smock described the open pit as:

… 115 feet deep and approximately 500 x 175 feet. The underground workings are south and southwest of it, and the ore has been followed for a distance of 900 feet, and to a depth of 185 feet ... The ore varies from a specular ore of metallic lustre and steel-gray shade of color to amorphous, compact masses of deep red. The crushed powder answers well as a paint, and stains deeply all with which it comes in contact. (Smock 1889, 45)

The Sterling mine was last worked between 1904 and 1910, when it finally closed due to a general decline in the economy and competition from the Mesabi Range in Minnesota. In the summer of 1942, the Rossie Iron Ore Company investigated the feasibility of using the ore to make iron-oxide pigments, and in 1948, the Republic Steel Corporation diamond drilled the property to determine what ore reserves might remain, but with discouraging results.

No one knows exactly when the locality was first noticed as a source of crystallized mineral specimens. Lewis Beck and Ebenezer Emmons reported hematite, quartz, siderite, and cacoxenite in their 1842 State reports, but it is Franklin B. Hough who is credited with the discovery of millerite at the Sterling mine in 1848— the first report of that mineral in the United States. Over the years, the locality has been visited by hundreds of mineral collectors who occasionally have been rewarded with specimens dug from the mine dumps that surround the old water-filled pit. Today the property is privately owned, and collecting is generally not permitted.

Fig. 127. Millerite. Sterling Mine, Antwerp, Jefferson Co. 4.9 cm fov. Steven C. Chamberlain collection. SCC

Geology and Origin

The origin of the Sterling mine hematite deposit and the interesting minerals it contains is complex and probably took place in several stages beginning in Precambrian time and continuing into the Paleozoic. The following synopsis is based on a combination of information gleaned from early studies, Republic Steel's diamond drill logs, and our own mineralogical investigation conducted in 1984. The Sterling mine orebody itself lies between Grenville Marble and a heavily chloritized pyritic gneiss that grades into a granitic gneiss, all of which dip to the northwest and are overlain by the Cambrian-age Potsdam Sandstone. In areas, the Potsdam Sandstone also shows replacement by hematite, proving iron mineralization was active at least into lower Paleozoic time. The major part of the hematite orebody probably formed when pyrite in the gneiss was oxidized by meteoric or hydrothermal waters, resulting in an acidic solution rich in iron that both chloritized the adjacent gneiss and reacted with the marble, replacing it with hematite. The intense chloritization of the gneiss was probably accompanied by considerable volume changes, resulting in a rock so heavily slickensided that it was once thought to be a new mineral, called "dysyntribite."

The minerals of collector interest occur in open cavities from 1 to 30 cm across in the massive red hematite ore. The presence of stilpnomelane and ferroan talc among these is significant, for they record an interesting geological event that occurred sometime after their formation. When checked with a magnet, most of the bladed "hematite" crystals at the Sterling mine are found to actually be magnetite pseudomorphs after hematite. Chemical analyses of the stilpnomelane and ferroan talc in direct association with the pseudomorphs show marked enrichment in ferric iron, suggesting a coupled oxidation-reduction reaction between these minerals. This reaction was probably driven by some regional tectonic event, though all the other nearby hematite mines in the Antwerp-Keene belt are devoid of these minerals. Their absence underscores the significance of the more diverse, chemically complex precursor lithologies originally present at the Sterling mine site, without which the mineral assemblages present could not have formed.

Minerals

There are sixteen mineral species currently known from the Sterling mine, all of which occur as specimens of interest to collectors. Three additional species have been reported but cannot be verified: cacoxenite (most likely a misidentification of stilpnomelane or goethite), ankerite (probably a misidentification of siderite-dolomite mixtures), and barite.

Fig. 128. Millerite. Sterling Mine, Antwerp, Jefferson Co. 3 cm spray. New York State Museum. JAS

Fig. 130. Pecoraite pseudomorphs after millerite. Sterling Mine, Antwerp, Jefferson Co. 2 cm fov. Canadian Museum of Nature. GWR

Fig. 129. Millerite. Sterling Mine, Antwerp, Jefferson Co. 3 cm fov. A. E. Seaman Mineral Museum. GWR

Fig. 131. Siderite. Sterling Mine, Antwerp, Jefferson Co. 4.5 cm fov. Root collection, New York State Museum. SCC

Apatite Group, $Ca_5(PO_4,CO_3)_3(OH,F)$, crystals occur sparingly in some cavities as drusy, pink to beige, tabular individuals, generally less than 0.5 mm in diameter scattered on quartz and magnetite pseudomorphs after hematite. Their X-ray powder pattern and slow effervescence in hydrochloric acid suggest they are probably a carbonate-rich variety.

Aragonite, $CaCO_3$, is rare at the Sterling mine, and forms spikey colorless to white crystals to 1 mm on quartz and magnetite pseudomorphs after hematite.

Calcite, $CaCO_3$, crystals are present in at least three generations: an early generation of scalenohedral crystals (often encrusted with stilpnomelane); a second generation of milky white, modified rhombohedral crystals; and a late generation of gray-white, "nailhead" habit crystals to ~1 cm in diameter.

Chalcopyrite, $CuFeS_2$, is another rare mineral at the Sterling mine, having been observed on only a few specimens as modified bisphenoidal crystals.

Dolomite, $Ca(Mg,Fe)(CO_3)_2$, is relatively common, and typically occurs as cream to tan colored spheroidal aggregates of curved rhombohedrons over a centimeter across. Electron microprobe analyses of the dolomite show it contains a significant amount of iron, and is often epitactically overgrown by golden brown to reddish brown siderite. Bulk wet-chemical analyses of such mixtures yield compositions resembling those of ankerite, which may explain the erroneous reports of that mineral from the Sterling mine.

Goethite, $FeO(OH)$, occurs as massive brown "limonite" as well as golden brown tufts of acicular crystals generally less than a millimeter across on quartz and other minerals in some cavities.

Hematite, Fe_2O_3, is abundant in earthy to rocky, brick-red masses and less so as globular, red-brown, botryoidal aggregates ("kidney ore"). The latter may have been more abundant when the mine was in operation, but is less so today, as its overall purity and high iron content would have made it prime ore. Hematite also forms small (1–3 mm), bladed, lustrous crystals or rosettes lining cavities in the massive ore, though most such specimens show partial to complete replacement by magnetite.

Magnetite, Fe_3O_4, is abundant as pseudomorphs after bladed hematite crystals, which are often associated with quartz, stilpnomelane, and dolomite, the four of which together are probably the most common minerals found at this locality.

Millerite, NiS, specimens from the Sterling mine are highly sought by collectors, because the best rank among the finest examples of that mineral known. Lustrous, radial aggregates of brassy, acicular crystals 1–3 cm across on a contrasting matrix of shiny, black magnetite pseudomorphs after hematite crystals or

sparkling crystals of quartz make impressive specimens indeed. At high-magnification, some individual millerite needles show spiral growth features, resulting in twisted crystals that resemble drill bits.

Fig. 132. *Siderite, quartz, magnetite pseudomorphs after hematite. Sterling Mine, Antwerp, Jefferson Co. 9.8 cm. Steven C. Chamberlain collection. MW*

Fig. 133. *Stilpnomelane. Sterling Mine, Antwerp, Jefferson Co. 6 cm fov. A. E. Seaman Mineral Museum. GWR*

Pecoraite, $Ni_3Si_2O_5(OH)_4$, forms brilliant yellow-green pseudomorphs after millerite crystal aggregates to 1 cm across.

Pyrite, FeS_2, occasionally forms 1–2 mm cubes or octahedra in some cavities, though of more interest to collectors are the rarer "rosettes" of octahedral crystals associated with siderite.

Quartz, SiO_2, is ubiquitous, forming drusy linings in nearly every crystal-lined cavity. The crystals, which are seldom greater than 0.5 cm, commonly occur as colorless equant crystals with more or less equally developed positive and negative rhombohedral faces, resembling hexagonal dipyramids.

Siderite, $FeCO_3$, is present in some vugs as either tan or red-brown rhombohedral crystals 1–5 mm across sometimes forming aggregates to several centimeters. Occasionally, crystals are seen impaled on needles of millerite or epitactically overgrowing ferroan dolomite.

Sphalerite, ZnS, is rare at the Sterling mine and has been observed on fewer than a half dozen specimens, including one in the Oren Root collection (formerly at Hamilton College, now at the New York State Museum), where it occurs as a single, 6 mm, resinous, brown, twinned crystal with siderite, dolomite, quartz, calcite, chalcopyrite, and magnetite pseudomorphs after hematite.

Stilpnomelane, $K(Fe,Al)_{10}Si_{12}O_{30}(OH)_{12}$, (originally known by the obsolete name "*chalcodite*") is relatively abundant and forms velvety, greenish brown aggregates of micaceous microcrystals several centimeters across. It is nearly always associated with the magnetite pseudomorphs after hematite, as each owes its existence to the other. The color and ferric iron content of the stilpnomelane correlate with the degree of hematite reduction to magnetite: green stilpnomelane tends to have less ferric iron and occurs with lightly to moderately reduced hematite, whereas golden brown stilpnomelane contains significantly more ferric iron and tends to occur with more heavily reduced, magnetite-rich specimens.

Talc, $(Mg,Fe)_3Si_4O_{10}(OH)_2$, forms gray, clay-like masses or gray-white spheroidal aggregates in some of the cavities. Chemical analyses show the talc contains a significant amount of iron, and like the stilpnomelane, probably played a similar role in the oxidation-reduction reaction involved with the observed replacement of hematite by magnetite.

Similar Occurrences

Dodge mine (44°21'31"N, 75°14'26"W); Chub Lake hematite prospect (44°19'56"N, 75°21'34"W); Pierrepont iron rose locality (44°30'46"N, 75°01'05"W); Toothaker Creek hematite locality (44°12'09"N, 75°18'30"W); Whitton prospect (44°12'57"N, 75°20'6"W); Bowman prospect (44°25'12"N, 75°17'14"W); Caledonia mine (44°16'34"N, 75°31'58"W); all the other hematite mines in the Antwerp-Keene belt.

References

BECK, L. (1842) *Mineralogy of New-York*. W. & A. White and J. Visscher, Albany, New York.

BUDDINGTON, A. F. (1934) Geology and mineral resources of the Hammond, Antwerp and Lowville quadrangles. *New York State Museum Bulletin No. 296*:202-27.

EMMONS, E. (1842) *Geology of New York, Part II, Survey of the Second Geological District*. W. & A. White and J. Visscher, Albany, New York.

HADDOCK, J. A. (1895) *The Growth of a Century as Illustrated in the History of Jefferson County, New York*. Weed-Parsons Printing Co., Albany, New York.

HOUGH, F. B. (1854) *A History of Jefferson County*. Sterling and Riddell, Watertown, New York.

HOUGH, F. B. and JOHNSON, S. W. (1850) On the discovery of sulphuret of nickel in northern New York. *American Journal of Science*, Series 2. 9:287-288.

ROBINSON, G. W. and CHAMBERLAIN, S. C. (1984) Famous mineral localities: The Sterling Mine, Antwerp, New York. *Mineralogical Record* 15:199-216.

Chub Lake Hematite Prospect

Significance

This small hematite deposit has produced many elegant quartz, hematite, and barite specimens, some of which are comparable to the world-class specimens from the iron mines in the western part of the Lakes District in Cumbria, England.

Location and History

The Chub Lake hematite prospect is on the Tessmer farm, about 150 meters north of the southwestern end of Chub Lake at 44°19'56"N, 75°21'34"W near the village of Hailesboro in the town of Fowler, St. Lawrence County, NY.

In 1853, Franklin Hough discussed the economic mineral resources of St. Lawrence County, and included an annotated list of minerals:

The *specular ores*, so called from the splendid luster of the crystals of Elba and other localities, occurs under two varieties, distinct in situation, and accompanying minerals. The least important of these is the *crystaline* variety, occurring in gneiss and white limestone, often beautifully crystallized in plates …

Quartz apparently in twelve sided crystals, formed by joining the bases of two six sided pyramids, but really having a short prism between, is usually found with this ore, and cavities lined with crystalline groups of these minerals, form splendid cabinet specimens. (Hough 1853, 683)

The mines of crystallized specular iron in Gouverneur, Fowler, Edwards and Hermon all afford splendid crystals. The iron mine near Chub Lake, in Fowler, afforded beautiful crystals, nearly transparent, and quite brilliant. (Hough 1853, 694)

Although many early specimens were simply labeled "Fowler," those from Chub Lake are distinctive and relatively common in older collections. Specimens in the Oren Root Collection were specifically labeled Chub Lake and were obtained from noted mineral collector and dealer Chester D. Nims around 1880. In 1882, the collector John H. Caswell obtained other Chub Lake specimens from Albert H. Chester of Hamilton College. Specimens entered many collections during the second half of the nineteenth century.

It appears the locality then languished in obscurity for the first half of the twentieth century. In the 1950s, a local physician-mineralogist collected some noteworthy specimens, but the locality then seems to have slipped back into obscurity. In 1983, in preparing for a lecture at the 10th Rochester Mineralogical Symposium, Steven C. Chamberlain and George W. Robinson visited the historic Oren Root Collection at Hamilton College and noted several outstanding hematite, quartz, and barite specimens labeled as being from Chub Lake. Later that year, Schuyler Alverson and George W. Robinson rediscovered the locality. Independently, Syracuse collector Ronald Waddell tracked down the owner of Chub Lake, Max Tessmer, who knew about the old iron prospect on his property, and thereby also rediscovered the locality, sharing it with William P. Dossert, Steven C. Chamberlain, and William S. Condon. In 1983, the dumps appeared largely undisturbed since the nineteenth century. For the next twenty years, Chub Lake was a popular collecting site. Local collectors, Robert Johnson, Charles Bowman, Eric Edie, Vernon Phillips, and others visited the site frequently. The dumps were completely turned over and outcroppings of the mineralization were uncovered and directly exploited. Mineral clubs and collectors from far and wide visited the locality and collected specimens. Today the locality is again infrequently visited.

Fig. 134. Barite. Chub Lake, Hailesboro, St. Lawrence Co. 3 cm. New York State Museum. JAS

Fig. 135. Hematite, quartz. Chub Lake, Hailesboro, St. Lawrence Co. 9 cm. Steven C. Chamberlain collection. SCC

Geology and Origin

The geology and origin of the Chub Lake prospect and other similar occurrences in St. Lawrence County have not been studied in any detail. The deposit sits at the boundary (an unconformity) between the Precambrian basement complex and the overlying Potsdam Sandstone. The host rocks include Grenville Marble and highly altered metamorphic rocks, now dark green. Some barite and quartz crystals are frozen in massive hematite and some quartz crystals are encased in finely granular marble, but most of the mineralization appears to have formed in open cavities long after the period of deep burial and tectonic activity that produced the regional metamorphism in the Precambrian. It is likely that iron-bearing meteoric water migrating along the basal unconformity deposited the observed mineralization in voids resulting from the dissolution of the original Grenville Marble. If so, the Chub Lake prospect is largely Paleozoic in age.

Minerals

Only four minerals are found in significant quantity at the Chub Lake prospect, but all occur in desirable crystallized specimens.

Barite, $BaSO_4$, occurs sparingly as transparent, yellow to golden yellow, prismatic crystals to 3 cm associated with quartz and hematite crystals, and as white blades to 5 cm frozen in fine-grained specular hematite. Sometimes the embedded barite has been dissolved away leaving crystal molds or has been replaced by quartz to form pseudomorphs.

Calcite, $CaCO_3$, forms creamy white crystals with frosted surfaces to 5 cm, most often on hematite crystals. Crystals are consistently scalenohedral with a rhombohedral modification at the termination, and appear late in the paragenetic sequence.

Hematite, Fe_2O_3, occurs as flattened rhombohedral crystals to 2 cm, usually with splendent luster. They form complex intergrowths and arrays lining cavities associated with quartz crystals, barite crystals, and calcite crystals. Hematite crystals form a number of different aggregates, including large hemispherical arrays of crystals to 9 cm across or as specimens with lustrous, crystal-lined surfaces exceeding 30 cm. Hematite also occurs as individual crystals and rosettes on or inside quartz crystals, and as fine-grained, dark gray masses containing embedded white barite or quartz crystals.

Fig. 136. Quartz, hematite. Chub Lake, Hailesboro, St. Lawrence Co.
10 cm. Steven C. Chamberlain collection. MW

Quartz, SiO_2, most commonly forms equant crystals dominated by equally developed positive and negative rhombohedra with only very minor prism faces, mimicking hexagonal dipyramids. Less commonly, they are elongated prisms. Individual crystals rarely exceed 5 cm, although crystal groups can be 10 cm or more. Some are transparent and colorless or pale smoky in color. Others are tan, brown, or black, and translucent to opaque. Many show phantoms of opaque, colored quartz within a transparent outer layer. "Sand crystals" appear to have formed in marble and include large volumes of fine calcite particles. When these have weathered free, they have no points of attachment and are porous, but still have sharp crystal faces. Tan quartz with a microplumose replacement texture also occurs as pseudomorphs after barite crystals embedded in massive hematite.

Similar Occurrences

Dodge mine (44°21'31"N, 75°14'26"W); Pierrepont Iron Rose locality (44°30'46"N, 75°01'05"W); Toothaker Creek prospect (44°12'09"N, 75°18'30"W); Whitton prospect (44°12'57"N, 75°20'6"W); Bowman prospect (44°25'12"N, 75°17'14"W); and others reported in the older literature, but now lost. Mines in the Antwerp-Keene belt, especially the Sterling mine (44°14'18"N, 75°35'28"W) and the Caledonia mine (44°16'34"N, 75°31'58"W) are almost certainly of similar origin, but have far more complex mineralogy.

References

HOUGH, F. B. (1853) *A History of St. Lawrence and Franklin Counties, New York: From the Earliest Period to the Present Time.* Little & Co., Albany. 719p.

LUPULESCU, M. (2008) Minerals from the iron deposits of New York State. *Rocks & Minerals* 83:248-266.

WALTER, M. (2007) *Field Collecting Minerals in the Empire State.* Privately published. 212p.

Zinc Mines of the Balmat-Edwards Mining District

Significance

The zinc mines of the Balmat-Edwards mining district are noteworthy because the original sulfides that comprise the ore were deposited by Precambrian black smokers on the sea floor and they have since undergone a long and complex geologic history that resulted in unique mineral assemblages. Collectors prize the well-formed crystals that occurred in fractures that were mineralized by hydrothermal solutions. These include fine specimens of calcite, sphalerite, tetrahedrite, anhydrite, barite, and celestine, in addition to cubic and tetrahexahedral crystals of magnetite that rank among the best in the world for that species. The mines are the only source for significant specimens of precious metals (silver) in New York State.

Location and History

The Balmat-Edwards mining district comprises a number of zinc and talc deposits that stretches across St. Lawrence County in an approximately twenty-five-mile-long, NE-SW trending belt from Balmat at its southern end, through Fowler, Talcville, and Edwards, and continuing on to West Pierrepont at its northern end. A number of zinc prospects and mines are sited along this belt, of which the following are probably those of greater interest to mineral collectors: the Zinc Corporation of America (ZCA) (formerly St. Joe Lead) No. 2 and 3 mines at Balmat (44°16'21"N, 75°24'01"W) and (44°16'00"N, 75°24'10"W); the ZCA Number 4 mine near Sylvia Lake (44°15'08"N, 75°24'11"W); the Hyatt mine near Talcville (44°18'12"N, 75°19'23"W); and ZCA's mine southwest of Pierrepont (44°30'32"N, 75°01'49"W).

Fig. 137. Calcite, goethite, hematite. ZCA #3 Mine, Balmat, St. Lawrence Co. 11 cm. Steven C. Chamberlain collection. SCC

The discovery of sphalerite in the district was first made on the Balmat farm, near Sylvia Lake, circa 1835, and noted in Ebenezer Emmons' 1838 report on the state's second geological district (though reported erroneously as "Belmont" farm). Whether zinc was not considered of great value in those times, or none of the small-scale test pits sunk on surface showings of sphalerite produced any sufficiently rich ore, it wasn't until 1915 before any significant interest was shown in mining zinc. In that year, the Northern Ore Company opened a mine at Edwards, followed by the Dominion Company of Gouverneur exploring the area around Sylvia Lake and at the Hyatt mine near Talcville, which was leased to the Hyatt Ore Corporation in 1918, that developed it into the second major producer in the district. In the early 1920s, St. Joe Mineral Corporation bought out the Northern Ore Company (then renamed New York Zinc Company), and continued operating the Edwards mine while developing others at Balmat. In 1987, Zinc Corporation of America (ZCA) bought out St. Joe's properties, but due to labor disputes and fluctuating prices of zinc, only worked them sporadically. In 2003, ZCA sold their Balmat mine and concentrator to HudBay Minerals Inc., which continued operations until August 2008, when they, too, were forced to shut down due to the falling price of zinc and continued high operating costs. Today a small crew remains at the mine to maintain the facility in hope that more favorable economics will one day return and mining will once again resume.

Over the past 140 years, many collectors have visited and collected interesting specimens from the dumps of both the talc and zinc mines across the district, but undoubtedly the finest specimens of sphalerite, magnetite, calcite, and other well-crystallized hydrothermal minerals were those collected from the underground workings by the miners and geologists. Among those who played an active role in preserving these specimens were Perry Caswell, who recovered huge calcite crystals (to several hundred pounds) from the St. Joe Lead No. 2 ½ mine at Balmat, and Bob Johnson and Ivan MacIntosh, who each ran local rock shops specializing in Balmat minerals in the 1970s and 1980s. Some of the finest calcites, sphalerites, and tetrahedrites known from the ZCA mines at Balmat were collected by Vernon Phillips circa 1980, as well as Charlie Bowman and other miners. Through the collecting efforts of William deLorraine, John Johnson, Gary Stacy, David Nace, Charles, Chuck, and David Bowman, Terry Holmes, and other miners, hundreds of world-class magnetite specimens encountered in the ZCA No. 4 mine were preserved. Were it not for these individuals and a liberal collecting policy allowed by St. Joe Minerals and ZCA, none of these treasured specimens would have been saved for future generations to study and enjoy.

Geology and Origin

The geology of the Balmat-Edwards district is extremely complex due to multiple episodes of structural deformation. The district lies within a sequence of Precambrian metasedimentary rocks of the Grenville Series: predominantly marble and tremolite schist with local bands of anhydrite and talc in the vicinity of the zinc and talc mines, and various quartzites, calc-silicate schists, and gneisses elsewhere. The original source of the sulfide ore is thought to be hydrothermal sea floor venting (black smokers) that resulted in a volcanogenic exhalative massive sulfide deposit that has since been sheared, folded, remobilized, and recrystallized multiple times under metamorphic conditions reaching upper amphibolite to lower granulite facies. It is believed that the hydrothermal minerals described below probably formed where fluids were available locally to carry dissolved minerals into fractures and gash veins where conditions were conducive to the growth of well-crystallized minerals as the solutions cooled, and/or reacted with adjacent rocks or mixed with other solutions.

Minerals

Because the Balmat-Edwards district includes a number of mines spread over a broad geographic area, it is not surprising that taken together they have produced a considerable number of different minerals (eighty-seven in all). These include species that occur in the host metasedimentary rocks, those found in the talc and sphalerite orebodies, as well as hydrothermally derived minerals. While the Balmat-Edwards district could serve well as an example of a crystalline rock-hosted mineral occurrence, here we will focus only on the hydrothermal minerals that occur as well-formed crystals in open pockets and seams. In addition to the fourteen species described below, a small, isolated occurrence of orpiment and realgar in small, rounded, anhedral to subhedral crystals was encountered in the early 1980s in the ZCA No. 2 mine at Balmat, as was an equally small occurrence of tiny pyrargyrite crystals on the 900 level of the No. 3 mine that exploited the Loomis orebody. Because so little material was available, only a few reference-grade specimens are known, and will not be further described here. Likewise, the large plates of colorless, prismatic gypsum crystals ("selenite") seen on the market around 1980 were found in an underground sump, and are clearly of post-mining origin and therefore not described.

Anhydrite, $CaSO_4$, occurs in tonnages as granular marble-like units in ZCA's mines at both Balmat and Edwards. Locally, transparent blue to purple cleavages up to ten or more centimeters across are encountered.

Fig. 138. Celestine. ZCA #3 Mine, Balmat, St. Lawrence Co. 8 cm. Steven C. Chamberlain collection. SCC

the district. Most crystals are colorless to gray-white, or occasionally pale lavender in color, and vary in size from microscopic to over 500 pounds in weight. The predominant crystal habits tend to be combinations of scalenohedral and rhombohedral forms with or without basal pinacoids, and twinned crystals are relatively common, including spindle-shaped colorless twins to 6 cm twinned on (02 21) from the St. Joe Lead No. 3 mine. Excellent specimens have been found on the 900 level of the ZCA No. 3 mine, in both the Loomis and Gleason orebodies. Particularly fine, twinned, rhombohedral crystals of Iceland spar were found in G36 stope on the 500 level of the St. Joe Lead Co. No. 2 ½ mine at Balmat. In the 1960s, this same area, and on the 900 level below it, produced individual, etched, twinned crystals of Iceland spar over half a meter across. These were encountered in a watercourse, and recovered by Perry Caswell, who worked at the mine. Though etched with rough surfaces, the interiors of these crystals were remarkably clear and free of fractures, making desirable specimens as cleaved rhombohedrons to mineral collectors, and facet rough to gem cutters. Fine specimens of calcite have also been recovered from both the ZCA No. 4 mine at Sylvia Lake and the Hyatt mine near Talcville.

Celestine, $SrSO_4$, forms radial sprays and aggregates of intergrown, jack-straw habit gray-white crystals somewhat resembling cerussite. Groups of such crystals over 30 cm across were found with the huge calcite crystals described above from the St. Joe Lead Co. No. 2 ½ mine at Balmat.

Chalcopyrite, $CuFeS_2$, occurs as small, brassy, bisphenoidal crystals often perched on calcite crystals. Attractive specimens have been found on the 900 level of the ZCA No. 3 mine at Balmat.

Dufrénoysite, $Pb_2As_2S_5$, is a rare sulfosalt mineral, seldom found in well-formed crystals. The best-known specimens are probably those from the Lengenbach quarry in the Binn Valley, Wallis (Valais), Switzerland. Only a single specimen is known from the Balmat-Edwards District, and would not be included here, were it not for its extraordinarily high quality—perhaps the finest known from North America.

Hematite, Fe_2O_3, is occasionally observed as lustrous, bladed, black crystals a few millimeters across with colorless crystals of quartz and yellow-brown sphalerite. It was more prevalent on specimens from the mines operated by St. Joe Lead in Balmat in the 1960s–70s than it is on specimens collected in more recent years.

Magnetite, Fe_3O_4, is perhaps today the single, best-known mineral from the district among mineral collectors. This is due to the spectacular find of lustrous, well-formed, cubic and tetrahexahedral crystals made at the ZCA No. 4 mine in the Fowler orebody in 1991–92.

Sharp, colorless to white, pinacoidal crystals to 7 cm long were found associated with cubic magnetite crystals, colorless sphalerite, and halite in the F-24 stope (Fowler orebody) on the 2500 level of the ZCA No. 4 mine near Sylvia Lake. Unfortunately overshadowed by the magnetite, these anhydrite crystals are also significant, as some are among the best ever found in the United States.

Barite, $BaSO_4$, occurs as tabular gray-white crystals to nearly 10 cm across. Some examples that are stained with red hematite and sprinkled with microcrystals of pyrite or chalcopyrite make handsome specimens. Fine barite crystals were encountered in the early 1980s in the Loomis orebody on the 900 level of the ZCA No. 3 mine at Balmat.

Calcite, $CaCO_3$, is probably the most widespread of all the collectible hydrothermal minerals throughout

Fig. 139. Dufrénoysite, calcite. ZCA Mines, Balmat, St. Lawrence Co. 1.2 cm crystal. Canadian Museum of Nature. GWR

Fig. 140. Magnetite. ZCA #4 Mine, Balmat, St. Lawrence Co. 4 cm. Steven C. Chamberlain collection. SCC

The exact locality, now essentially mined out, was the F-24 stope, just below the 2500-foot top mining sublevel ([44°16'21"N, 75°24'11"W], 688 meters below the surface). The magnetite crystals, the best of which rank among the finest known, occurred by the thousands in a highly unusual, hydrothermally altered zone, and were associated with talc, colorless sphalerite, anhydrite, and

halite—an assemblage that appears unique in the world. While most crystals were less than 1 cm, many were 1–2 cm across, and a few reached 3 cm. Groups of intergrown crystals formed aggregates up to 25 cm across, though the best were generally less than half that size. Literally thousands of specimens were collected and distributed, ensuring Balmat will be forever known among collectors as a world-class magnetite locality.

Pyrite, FeS_2, is a common associate mineral in the massive sphalerite ore throughout the Balmat-Edwards district. It also occurs sparingly as a dusting of tiny crystals on earlier-formed calcite and barite crystals at the ZCA No. 3 and other mines at Balmat, but perhaps the most interesting specimens were found at the ZCA Pierrepont mine, where lustrous spherical aggregates from 2–20 cm in diameter were found in an altered metasedimentary layer next to the ore body. Although these probably originally formed as biogenic pyrite in a sedimentary rock, they have been subsequently metamorphosed and recrystallized by local hydrothermal activity.

Quartz, SiO_2, forms colorless prismatic crystals associated with sphalerite and occasional hematite that were found in the 1960s at the St. Joe mines at Balmat.

Silver, Ag, occurs very rarely as metallic sheets containing detectable amounts of mercury in gash veins associated with quartz, diopside, galena, and various lead-rich sulfosalts.

Sphalerite, ZnS, forms lustrous, complex crystals to 3 cm in fracture zones in a number of the ZCA mines throughout the district. Many are transparent and of gem quality and occur in a variety of colors. Golden brown to honey-colored crystals have been found at the No. 2 and 3 mines in Balmat; slightly darker crystals, at the Pierrepont mine; golden yellow crystals, at the Hyatt mine, near Talcville; and sulfur-yellow crystals from the 1300 level of the No. 4 mine near Sylvia Lake. All these color variants occur in high-quality specimens, and are much sought after by collectors.

Tetrahedrite, $Cu_6Cu_4(Fe,Zn)_2(Sb,As)_4S_{13}$, is not common in the Balmat-Edwards district, but a few good specimens are known. The best of these were collected by Vernon Phillips around 1980 on the 900 level of the ZCA No. 3 mine, Loomis orebody, and consist of small aggregates of lustrous, centimeter-sized, modified tetrahedral crystals.

Similar Occurrences

While the adjacent talc mines share common host rocks and geological history with the zinc mines, they typically lack the sulfide ores and hydrothermal minerals derived from them. Thus, there are no other truly geologically similar occurrences with similar mineralization known in the state.

Fig. 141. Magnetite. ZCA #4 Mine, Balmat, St. Lawrence Co. 2.4 cm. Steven C. Chamberlain collection. SCC

Fig. 142. Magnetite. ZCA #4 Mine, Balmat, St. Lawrence Co. 9 cm. Steven C. Chamberlain collection. SCC

Fig. 143. Magnetite. ZCA #4 Mine, Balmat, St. Lawrence Co. 7.5 cm. Steven C. Chamberlain collection. SCC

Fig. 145. Sphalerite. ZCA Pierrepont Mine, Pierrepont, St. Lawrence Co. 5.5 cm. Steven C. Chamberlain collection. SCC

Fig. 146. Sphalerite. ZCA Mines, Balmat, St. Lawrence Co. 2.5 cm. Canadian Museum of Nature. JS

Fig. 147. Silver. ZCA #3 Mine, Balmat, St. Lawrence Co. 4.4 cm. Steven C. Chamberlain collection. SCC

Fig. 144. Magnetite. ZCA #4 Mine, Balmat, St. Lawrence Co. 3 cm. Steven C. Chamberlain collection. SCC

References

BROWN, J. S., and ENGEL, A. E. J. (1956). Revision of Grenville stratigraphy and structure in the Balmat-Edwards district, northwest Adirondacks. *Bulletin of the Geological Society of America.* 67:1599-1622.

CHAMBERLAIN, S. C. (1992) Tetrahedrite crystals from the zinc mines at Balmat, St. Lawrence County, New York, *Rocks & Minerals* 67:176-178.

CHAMBERLAIN, S. C., ROBINSON, G. W., LUPULESCU, M., MORGAN, T. C., JOHNSON, J. T., and deLORRAINE, W. F. (2008). Cubic and tetrahexahedral magnetite crystals from the Fowler orebody, Zinc Corporation of America No. 4 mine, Balmat, New York. *Rocks & Minerals,* 83:224-239.

CHAMBERLAIN, S. C., ROBINSON, G. W., LUPULESCU, M., MORGAN, T. C., JOHNSON, J. T., and deLORRAINE, W. F. (2010). Cubic magnetite crystals from Balmat, New York. *Mineralogical Record,* 41: 527-537.

CUSHING, H. P. and NEWLAND, D. H. (1925). Geology of the Gouverneur Quadrangle. *New York State Museum Bulletin No. 259,* 120p.

deLORRAINE, W. F. (1979). Geology of the Fowler orebody, Balmat # 4 mine, Northwest Adirondacks. University of Massachusetts, Department of Geology and Geography, master's thesis.

EMMONS, E. (1838). Report of the second geological district of the state of New York. *New York Geological Survey Annual Report No. 2,* 185-220.

JOHNSON, J. (1998). Zinc in the northlands: A historical perspective of the Balmat/Edwards district. *Matrix,* 6:124-130.

Ellenville Mine

Significance

The Ellenville mine is famous for its exquisite specimens of lustrous, colorless quartz crystals as well as large, sharp crystals of chalcopyrite and rare, but fine crystals of brookite. It is one of the oldest mineral localities in New York State.

Location and History

The Ellenville mine is located on Mine Lane in the village of Ellenville, in southwestern Ulster County (41°42'44"N, 74°22'55"W). The mine was opened by at least 1820, though mining in the general vicinity had commenced nearly a century earlier. It was worked by the North American Coal and Mining Company in the 1850s, the Union Lead Mining Company in the 1860s, and the Ellenville Zinc Company from 1902 to 1919,

and, therefore, has been variously known as the Ulster, Union, Ellenville, and Ellenville Zinc mine at different times during its history. Undoubtedly, fine specimens were produced throughout its operation, though perhaps many of the best quartz and chalcopyrite specimens were collected in the 1900s by P. Edwin Clark, a superintendent with the Ellenville Zinc mine. Many collectors have visited the dumps since then and have been rewarded with groups of quartz crystals up to half a meter in length. In 1941, Lenny Morgan collected a single, 2.2 cm Japan Law twin. In the 1970s, the Army Corps of Engineers excavated rock for road construction from the ledges adjacent to and above the main vein, where several large pockets of quartz crystals were encountered. A number of collectors were fortunate to have visited the site at this time, including one of the authors (GWR), who extracted over one hundred crystals from one such pocket, including a doubly terminated Herkimer diamond-like crystal approximately 10 x 15 cm, now in the collection of the Canadian Museum of Nature.

Geology and Origin

The Ellenville mine is one of several genetically related hydrothermal vein-type deposits that cut the middle Silurian sedimentary rocks that comprise the Shawangunk Mountains. The veins are thought to have been emplaced along faults and fissures during Alleghanian time. They are relatively simple mineralogically, and consist predominantly of quartz and minor amounts of pyrite, with sphalerite, galena, and chalcopyrite as the only minerals of economic interest.

Minerals

In 2007, Hawkins noted twenty-four species that have been reported from the Ellenville mine, most of which are of poor quality and occur only in small quantities or as microcrystals. Therefore, we will only describe the species of greatest interest to collectors: brookite, chalcopyrite, galena, pyrite, quartz, and sphalerite.

Brookite, TiO_2, is rare at this locality, and very few if any specimens have been collected since the closure of the mine. When present, the crystals typically form sharp, lustrous, tabular, prismatic, dark reddish brown individuals to 1 cm on quartz, resembling those from Tremadoc, Wales. One remarkable specimen in the Rutgers College Museum was described by Valiant in 1898 as "a mass of grit rock 7 x 10 inches ... completely covered with quartz crystals—a beautiful specimen in itself—scattered over the face of this are about one hundred brilliant black crystals of brookite ... each about ¼ inch in diameter." (Valiant 1898, 147)

Fig. 148. Brookite. Ellenville Lead Mine, Ellenville, Ulster Co. 1 cm. Union College. SCC

Fig. 150. Quartz (Japan law twin). Ellenville Lead Mine, Ellenville, Ulster Co. 2.2 cm. Steven C. Chamberlain collection. SCC

Fig. 151. Quartz, chalcopyrite. Ellenville Lead Mine, Ellenville, Ulster Co. 23 cm. New York State Museum. GBG

Fig. 149. Chalcopyrite, quartz. Ellenville Lead Mine, Ellenville, Ulster Co. 11.5 cm. New York State Museum. JAS

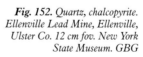

Fig. 152. Quartz, chalcopyrite. Ellenville Lead Mine, Ellenville, Ulster Co. 12 cm fov. New York State Museum. GBG

Chalcopyrite, $CuFeS_2$, is one of the minerals of primary interest, and occurs in well-formed crystals approaching 10 cm on quartz. The most common crystal forms are combinations of tetragonal disphenoids and scalenohedrons. Many crystals appear dark brown to black due to a coating of covellite, and often have chipped edges due to their inherent brittleness, making damage-free specimens highly valued by discriminating collectors.

Galena, PbS, specimens from Ellenville are relatively rare, and most often occur as cubes or octahedrons, or in combinations of those two forms, and seldom exceed 10 cm.

Pyrite, FeS_2, occurs as small, striated cubes to 1 cm with quartz.

Quartz, SiO_2, is perhaps the best-known mineral from Ellenville. It was the most abundant mineral in the vein, and thousands of crystals were collected and dispersed over the years. Most of these fall into one of two general types: the first consists of colorless, transparent, lustrous, prismatic crystals several centimeters in length, forming clusters over half a meter across; the second type tends to be larger overall, but more milky and equant. Type 2 crystals are frequently more distorted and occur as "floaters" in all sorts of unusual and often tabular shapes, which suggests they may be healed shards. A single Japan Law twin is at the New York State Museum. Valiant reported a single specimen of amethyst presumed to be from Ellenville, but this is unconfirmed.

Sphalerite, ZnS, occurs as reddish brown to nearly black crystals on quartz. In spite of its being the primary ore mineral mined, like galena, very few sphalerite specimens have been preserved.

Similar Occurrences

Spanish mine (Sun-Ray Tunnel) (near 41°43'01"N, 74°22'42"W); Red Bridge (Ulster, Spring Glen, Horseshoe) mine (41°39'33"N, 74°24'56"W).

References

HAWKINS, M. (2007). Ellenville, New York: A Classic Locality. *Rocks & Minerals* 82:508-15.

INGHAM, A. I. (1940). The zinc and lead deposits of Shawangunk Mountain, New York. *Economic Geology* 35:751-60.

VALIANT, W. S. (1898). An old mining region. *The Mineral Collector* 10:145-50.

Fig. 153. *Sphalerite, quartz. Ellenville Lead Mine, Ellenville, Ulster Co. 13 cm fov. Steven C. Chamberlain collection. SCC*